HOME BAKING

Edited by
Hilary Walden

CONTENTS

This edition first published 1978 by
Octopus Books Limited
59 Grosvenor Street, London W.1.

© 1978 Octopus Books Limited

ISBN 0 7064 0697 4

Produced and printed in Hong Kong by
Mandarin Publishers Limited
22a Westlands Road, Quarry Bay, Hong Kong

6 *Frontispiece:* WHOLEWHEAT BREAD *(page 20)*, POPPY SEED BREAD *(page 26)*,
MILK TWIST *(page 14)* AND WHITE BREAD *(page 11)* *(Photograph: RHM Foods Ltd)*

Weights and Measures

All measurements in this book are based on Imperial weights and measures, with American equivalents given in parenthesis.

Measurements in *weight* in the Imperial and American system are the same. Measurements in *volume* are different, and the following table shows the equivalents:

Spoon measurements

Imperial	U.S.
1 tablespoon	1 tablespoon
1½ tablespoons	2 tablespoons
2 tablespoons	3 tablespoons (abbrev: T)

Level spoon measurements are used in all the recipes.

Liquid measurements

1 Imperial pint	20 fluid ounces
1 American pint	16 fluid ounces
1 American cup	8 fluid ounces

American Ingredients

Commercially prepared 'mixed spice' is included in several recipes. If unobtainable blend together a selection of ground spices, such as nutmeg, cinnamon, mace and ginger and use instead.

If fresh yeast is not available substitute dry yeast, but use only half of the quantity recommended in the recipe: $2 \times \frac{1}{4}$ oz. packages dry yeast are equivalent to 1 cake compressed yeast.

INTRODUCTION

There can be nothing more satisfying than the delicious aroma and flavour of home-baked bread and yeast cakes. Yet, too few of us practise the art of yeast cooking today. Home baking is not the difficult, time-consuming task it is often thought to be and the results taste far better than commercially produced bread, to which we are so accustomed.

Successful bread-making depends partly on understanding the use of basic ingredients, particularly yeast and flour.

Yeast: Some supermarkets, private bakers and health food shops supply fresh (compressed) yeast but it is not always easy to obtain and dried yeast will give equally good results providing the manufacturer's directions are carefully followed.

When using dried yeast instead of fresh (compressed) yeast it is important to remember that dried yeast is more concentrated: ½ oz. dried yeast is equivalent to 1 oz. fresh yeast. If too much yeast is used the bread or yeast cakes will stale very quickly.

Dried yeast must first be dissolved in some of the warm liquid from the recipe, with ½-1 teaspoon sugar added. This yeast liquid is left in a warm place for 10-15 minutes or until frothy, then added to the dry ingredients.

Flour: Stronger flours, sometimes called bread flours, are ideal for yeast cookery. These have a higher gluten content and absorb more water to yield a firm elastic dough on kneading and a lighter open-textured bread.

Brown bread has a closer texture than white bread and a characteristic nutty flavour due to the wheatgerm contained. Wholemeal or wholewheat flour contains the whole grain of the wheat. It may be either stoneground or roller-milled. The former is more expensive but yields a better flavour. Wheatmeal flour contains 80-90% of the wheat grain, which includes all the wheatgerm and some bran.

Kneading dough: This is an important stage of bread-making because it strengthens the dough and develops elasticity. Kneading is generally carried out on a lightly floured surface. The dough is folded in half, pushed firmly with the heel of the hand and given a quarter-turn. This process is repeated until the dough is smooth, elastic and no longer sticky.

Some electric mixers have a dough hook attachment which can be used on a slow speed for kneading.

Rising dough: After kneading, the dough must be covered and set aside to rise. The temperature will affect the rising time. It may take 45-60 minutes in a warm place or up to 2 hours at room temperature (68°F). Ideally the dough should be allowed to rise slowly over a long period.

Shaping and proving dough: The risen dough must be kneaded again or 'knocked back' to ensure a good rise and even texture. Shape the dough as required, place on baking sheets or in tins, cover and leave to rise. This second rising is also known as 'proving'.

Baking: As a general rule, all yeast mixtures are baked in a hot oven, but the temperature is slightly lower for enriched doughs. To test a loaf, tap firmly on the base with the knuckles. If the loaf sounds hollow, it is cooked.

CRUMPETS *(page 44) (Photograph: McDougalls Country Life Flour)*

LOAVES AND ROLLS

Short Time Method White Bread

1 oz. (1 cake) fresh (compressed)
  yeast
½ pint + 6 tablespoons (1 ¾ cups)
  warm water
25 mg. tablet ascorbic acid

1 ½ lb. (6 cups) strong plain
  (all-purpose) flour
2 teaspoons salt
¼ oz. (½T) lard (shortening)
milk to glaze

Cream the yeast with 2 tablespoons (3T) of the water. Dissolve the ascorbic acid in the yeast liquid. Sift the flour and salt into a warmed bowl and rub in the lard. Make a well in the centre and pour in the yeast liquid and remaining water. Work to a stiff dough that leaves the sides of the bowl clean.

   Turn onto a lightly floured surface and knead thoroughly until the dough is smooth, elastic and no longer sticky. Shape into a ball, place in a bowl, cover and leave for 5 minutes.

   With the point of a sharp knife, cut a cross on the top of the loaf and glaze with milk. Place on a baking sheet and put inside a lightly oiled polythene (plastic) bag. Leave in a warm place until doubled in size, about 45-50 minutes. Remove from the bag.

   Bake in a hot oven, 425°F, Gas Mark 7 for 45-50 minutes or until the loaf sounds hollow when tapped underneath. Cool on a wire rack.
Makes one 2 lb. loaf

Basic White Bread

3 lb. (12 cups) strong plain
  (all-purpose) flour
3-4 teaspoons salt
1 oz. (2T) lard (shortening) or
  margarine
1 oz. (1 cake) fresh (compressed)
  yeast

1½ pints (3¾ cups) warm water
Glaze:
1 egg, beaten with a little milk, or
  salted water

Sift the flour and salt together into a bowl. Rub in the fat. Blend the yeast with 4 tablespoons (⅓ cup) of the water. Make a well in the centre of the flour and pour in the yeast liquid and remaining water. Using one hand, draw the ingredients together and work to a firm dough, until the mixture comes cleanly away from the sides of the bowl.

Turn onto a lightly floured surface and knead thoroughly for 10 minutes until the dough is smooth and elastic. Shape into a ball and place in a clean bowl. Cover with a damp cloth and leave to rise in a warm place for about 1½ hours or until doubled in size.

Turn onto a lightly floured surface and knead for 5 minutes. For two 2 lb. tin loaves, divide the dough into 2 equal portions. To make four 1 lb. tin loaves divide into 4 portions. Shape each piece of dough into an oblong, the same width as the tin. Place the dough in greased 2 lb. or 1 lb. loaf tins, tucking the ends underneath.

Place each tin inside an oiled polythene (plastic) bag and leave in a warm place for about 1 hour until the dough has risen to the top of the tins. Remove the polythene bag. Brush the loaves with egg glaze or salted water. Bake in a hot oven, 450°F, Gas Mark 8 for 30-40 minutes for 1 lb. loaves, 45-55 minutes for 2 lb. loaves. The bread should sound hollow when tapped underneath. For a crustier loaf, turn the cooked bread out onto a baking sheet and bake for a further 10 minutes.

Cool on a wire rack.

Makes four 1 lb. loaves or two 2 lb. loaves

The bread dough can be used to make a variety of loaves. For the following, prepare the basic dough and follow the above recipe to the shaping stage.

Cob:
Divide the dough in half and shape each piece to a smooth round. Place on a floured baking sheet and dust with flour. Rise and bake as above.

Cottage loaf:
Break off one quarter of the dough and form into a smooth ball. Form the remainder into a larger ball and place on a floured baking sheet. Put the small ball of dough on top and push a floured finger through the centre of the loaf. Rise and bake as above.

Farmhouse loaf:
Shape the dough to fit loaf tins. Place in the tins and make a lengthwise cut through the top of the dough with a sharp knife. Rise and bake as above.

Bread Rolls

1 lb. (4 cups) strong plain
(all-purpose) flour
1 teaspoon salt
½ oz. (2T) lard

½ pint (1 ¼ cups) warm water
Glaze:
beaten egg or salted water
poppy seeds (optional)

Prepare the dough to the initial rising stage, as for Basic white bread (see page 11). Turn the risen dough onto a lightly floured surface and knead for 5 minutes. Divide into 12 equal pieces.

Roll each piece of dough to a ball. Place on floured baking sheets. Put into polythene (plastic) bags and leave to rise in a warm place for 40 minutes or until doubled in size.

Brush the rolls with beaten egg or salted water and sprinkle with poppy seeds, if liked. Bake in a hot oven, 450°F, Gas Mark 8 for about 20 minutes. Transfer to a wire rack to cool.

Makes 12 rolls

Alternatively the pieces of dough may be shaped into fancy rolls as suggested below.

Cottage rolls:

Break off one quarter of each piece of dough and form into a tiny smooth ball. Form the remainder into larger balls and place on a floured baking sheet. Put the small balls of dough on top and push a floured finger through the centre of each roll. Rise and bake as above.

Knots:

Shape each piece of dough into a long roll, about 5 inches long. Tie a knot in the centre and place on a floured baking sheet. Rise and bake as above.

Plait rolls:

Divide each portion of dough into 3 and roll into thin strands, about 5 inches long. Gather one end of each of the 3 strands together and plait the loose ends, crossing each strand alternately. Finally gather the short ends together. Place the rolls on a floured baking sheet, rise and bake as above.

BASIC WHITE BREAD *(page 11)*

Milk Twist

½ oz. (½ cake) fresh (compressed) yeast
½ pint (1¼ cups) warm milk
1 lb. (4 cups) strong plain (all-purpose) flour
2 teaspoons salt

½ oz. (1T) lard (shortening)
Glaze:
1 egg, beaten
1 tablespoon coarse sea salt or wheat flakes

Cream the yeast with 2 tablespoons (3T) of the milk. Sift the flour and salt into a warmed bowl and rub in the lard. Make a well in the centre and pour in the yeast liquid and remaining milk. With one hand or a spatula, draw all the ingredients together and beat until the mixture comes cleanly away from the sides of the bowl.

Turn onto a lightly floured surface and knead well for 10 minutes. Place in a clean bowl, cover with a damp cloth and leave in a warm place for 1½ hours or until doubled in size.

Turn onto a lightly floured surface and knead for 5 minutes. Divide into two and shape each piece of dough into a roll, about 14 inches long. Press one end of each strand together and seal with a little of the beaten egg. Twist the strands together to form a loaf and seal the short ends with beaten egg.

Place on a greased baking sheet and put inside an oiled polythene (plastic) bag. Leave in a warm place for 30 minutes or until doubled in size. Remove from the bag.

Brush with the egg and sprinkle with the sea salt or wheat flakes. Bake in a moderately hot oven, 400°F, Gas Mark 6 for 30-35 minutes until golden brown. Turn onto a wire rack to cool.
Makes one 1 lb. loaf

Granary Bread

1 oz. (1 cake) fresh (compressed)
  yeast
1 oz. (1½T) malt extract
½ pint (1¼ cups) warm water

2 lb. (8 cups) granary flour
1 tablespoon salt
1½ tablespoons (2T) corn oil

Cream yeast with the malt extract and 4 tablespoons (⅓ cup) of the water. Place flour and salt in a warmed bowl and make a well in the centre. Pour in the yeast mixture, oil and remaining water. Work the ingredients together to form a firm smooth dough.

Turn onto a floured surface and knead for 8-10 minutes. Place in a clean bowl and cover with a damp cloth. Leave in a warm place for 1-1½ hours until doubled in size.

Turn onto a floured surface and knead for 5 minutes. Divide the dough in half and roll each piece into a smooth ball. Place on a greased baking sheet. Put inside an oiled polythene (plastic) bag and leave in a warm place for 45 minutes. Remove from the bag. Bake in a hot oven, 450°F, Gas Mark 8 for 10 minutes.

Reduce temperature to moderately hot, 400°F, Gas Mark 6 and bake for 30-35 minutes. Turn onto a wire rack to cool. Serve sliced and buttered.

Makes two 7-8 inch round loaves

Caraway Bread

¾ oz. (¾ cake) fresh (compressed)
  yeast
1 pint (2½ cups) warm milk
1 lb. (4 cups) wholemeal
  (wholewheat) flour

1 lb. (4 cups) medium rye flour
1½ teaspoons salt
1½ oz. (¼ cup) soft (light) brown
  sugar
2 teaspoons caraway seeds

Blend yeast with 2 tablespoons (3T) of the milk. Mix the flours, salt and sugar in a warmed bowl. Make a well in the centre and pour in the yeast liquid and remaining milk. Draw the dry ingredients into the liquid and beat until a smooth dough is formed.

Turn onto a lightly floured surface and knead for 10 minutes until the dough becomes elastic. Place in a bowl, cover with a damp cloth and leave in a warm place for 1-1½ hours until doubled in bulk.

Turn onto a floured surface and knead in the caraway seeds. Cut the dough in half and form each piece into a loaf shape. Place in greased 1 lb. loaf tins, cover with a damp cloth and leave in a warm place for 35-45 minutes or until risen to the top of the tins.

Bake in the centre of a very hot oven, 475°F, Gas Mark 9 for 15 minutes. Lower the temperature to hot, 425°F, Gas Mark 7 and put the tins on a lower shelf. Bake for a further 25-30 minutes or until the bread sounds hollow when tapped underneath. Cool on a wire tray.

Makes two 1 lb. loaves

Wheatmeal Bread

½ oz. (½ cake) fresh (compressed) yeast
¾ pint (2 cups) warm water
12 oz. (3 cups) wholemeal (wholewheat) flour
12 oz. (3 cups) strong plain (all-purpose) flour, sifted
1 teaspoon salt
½ oz. (1T) lard (shortening)
cracked wheat (optional)

Cream the yeast with 4 tablespoons (⅓ cup) of the water. Place the flours and salt in a warmed bowl and rub in the lard. Make a well in the centre and pour in the yeast liquid and remaining water. With one hand or a spatula, draw all the ingredients together and beat until the mixture comes cleanly away from the sides of the bowl.

Turn onto a lightly floured surface and knead well for 2 minutes until the dough is smooth and elastic but fairly soft. Shape into a smooth round. (For alternative shapes, see below and page 11). Scatter with cracked wheat or flour. Place on a greased baking sheet. Put inside an oiled polythene (plastic) bag and leave in a warm place for 1½ hours or until doubled in size. Remove from the bag.

Bake in a hot oven, 450°F, Gas Mark 8 for 40-45 minutes until evenly browned. Transfer to a wire rack to cool completely before serving.
Makes one 9 inch round loaf

Flowerpot wheatmeal loaves:
Prepare the wheatmeal dough as above. Divide the dough in half. Shape each piece into a ball and place in well-greased clay flower pots, approximately 5 inches in diameter across the top. Brush the tops with a little salted water and sprinkle with cracked wheat. Rise and bake as above, reducing the baking time to 30-40 minutes.

Bread Sticks

¾ oz. (¾ cake) fresh (compressed)
 yeast
¾ pint (2 cups) warm milk
1 ½ lb. (6 cups) strong plain
 (all-purpose) flour

2 teaspoons salt
2 oz. (¼ cup) butter, melted

Blend yeast with 3 tablespoons (¼ cup) of the milk. Sift flour and salt into a bowl. Make a well in the centre and pour in the yeast liquid and remaining milk. Draw enough of the flour into the liquid to make a thick batter. Sprinkle the top with a little flour and leave in a warm place for 15-20 minutes until spongy.

Pour the melted butter onto the yeast mixture. Draw the rest of the flour into the centre and mix thoroughly to form a smooth elastic dough. Turn onto a floured surface and knead for 5 minutes. Place in a bowl, cover with a damp cloth and leave in a warm place for 1 hour.

Turn onto a floured surface and knead for 5-7 minutes. Break into small pieces and shape into sticks, 6-8 inches long and about 1 inch thick. Place on a greased baking sheet and leave to rise in a warm place for 15 minutes.

Bake in a moderately hot oven, 400°F, Gas Mark 6 for 10 minutes, then reduce the temperature to moderate, 350°F, Gas Mark 4 and bake for a further 20-25 minutes until golden brown. Cool on a wire tray.
Makes about 40 bread sticks

Wholewheat Splits

1 oz. (1 cake) fresh (compressed)
 yeast
½ pint (1 ¼ cups) warm water and
 milk, mixed
1 lb. (4 cups) wholemeal
 (wholewheat) flour

1 lb. (4 cups) strong plain
 (all-purpose) flour, sifted
1 teaspoon salt
½ oz. (1T) lard (shortening),
 melted

Cream the yeast with 3 tablespoons (¼ cup) of the liquid. Mix the flours and salt together in a warmed bowl and make a well in the centre. Pour in the yeast, lard and remaining liquid. Draw enough flour into the liquid to form a thick batter. Sprinkle some of the flour over this mixture and leave in a warm place for about 45 minutes, until spongy.

Do not knead, but mix together with a spoon or knife to the consistency of a soft paste. Dust with flour and leave for 30 minutes in a warm place until well risen.

Turn onto a floured surface and roll lightly to a square, about 1 inch thick. Place on a greased baking sheet and put into an oiled polythene (plastic) bag. Leave for about 15 minutes. Remove from the bag.

Bake in a moderately hot oven, 400°F, Gas Mark 6 for 15-20 minutes. Cool on a wire tray. When cold, cut into squares. Serve, split and buttered.
Makes about 25 splits

Stoneground Wholewheat Bread

½ oz. (½ cake) fresh (compressed)
  yeast
¾ pint (2 cups) warm water
1½ lb. (6 cups) stoneground
  wholemeal (wholewheat) flour

2 teaspoons rock salt
1 tablespoon clear honey
1½ teaspoons oil

Cream the yeast with 2 tablespoons (3T) of the water. Place flour and salt in a warmed bowl, make a well in the centre and pour in the yeast liquid, honey, oil and remaining water. Draw the ingredients together and beat until the dough comes cleanly away from the sides of the bowl.

Turn onto a floured surface and knead for 8 minutes until smooth and elastic. Place in a bowl, cover with a damp cloth and leave in a warm place for 1½ hours or until doubled in bulk.

Knead vigorously for 10 minutes on a floured surface. Divide in half and form each piece of dough into a round. With the point of a sharp knife, mark a cross on the top. Place on a greased baking sheet. Put inside an oiled polythene (plastic) bag and leave in a warm place for 30-45 minutes until well risen. Remove from the bag.

Dust with a little wholemeal flour and bake in a very hot oven, 475°F, Gas Mark 9 for 15 minutes. Reduce the temperature to hot, 425°F, Gas Mark 7 and lower the shelf. Continue to bake for 25-30 minutes. Cool on a wire rack.

Makes two 7-8 inch round loaves

Wholewheat Bread

¾ oz. (¾ cake) fresh (compressed)
  yeast
¾ pint + 3 tablespoons (2¼ cups)
  warm water
2 lb. (8 cups) wholemeal
  (wholewheat) flour

1 teaspoon salt
2 oz. (⅓ cup) soft (light) brown
  sugar

Cream the yeast with 3 tablespoons (¼ cup) of the water. Place the flour and salt in a warmed bowl and stir in the sugar. Make a well in the centre and pour in the yeast and remaining liquid. Draw the ingredients together and beat until the dough comes away from the sides of the bowl.

Turn onto a lightly floured surface and knead for 8 minutes to give a smooth, elastic dough. Place in a clean bowl, cover with a damp cloth and leave in a warm place for 1½ hours or until doubled in bulk.

Turn onto a lightly floured surface and knead again for 5-7 minutes. Shape into a loaf and place in a greased 2 lb. loaf tin. (For alternative shapes, see below and page 11). Put into an oiled polythene (plastic) bag and leave in a warm place to rise for 30-45 minutes until doubled in bulk. Remove from the bag.

Bake in a hot oven, 450°F, Gas Mark 8 for 15 minutes. Lower the temperature to moderately hot, 400°F, Gas Mark 6, put the bread on a lower shelf and bake for a further 30-35 minutes.

Turn out and cool on a wire rack. Serve either warm or cold.
Makes one 2 lb. loaf

Wholewheat plait:
Prepare the wholewheat dough as above. Divide the risen dough into 3 equal pieces. Roll each piece into a long strand, gather one end of each strand and plait the loose ends. Gather the short ends together. Place the plait on a greased baking sheet and sprinkle with poppy seeds. Rise and bake as above.

Wholewheat rolls:
Prepare the wholewheat dough as above. Divide the risen dough into 24 equal sized pieces. Shape into plain or fancy rolls, such as cottage rolls, plaits and knots (as described on page 12). Place on a greased baking sheet and sprinkle with poppy seeds, if liked. Cover with a sheet of oiled polythene (plastic) and leave to rise in a warm place for 30 minutes or until doubled in size. Remove from the bag. Bake in a hot oven, 450°F, Gas Mark 8 for about 20 minutes until brown.

WHOLEWHEAT BREAD *(Photograph: Van den Berghs)*

Russian Black Bread

¾ oz. (¾ cake) fresh (compressed)
  yeast
½ pint + 2 tablespoons (1⅓ cups)
  warm water
2 tablespoons (3T) clear honey
3 tablespoons (¼ cup) black
  treacle (molasses)
1 oz. (2T) wheatgerm

6 oz. (1½ cups) strong plain
  (all-purpose) flour
12 oz. (3 cups) rye flour
1½ teaspoons salt
1 teaspoon ground coriander
1 teaspoon ground cinnamon
2 oz. (¼ cup) butter, melted
oil for brushing

Cream the yeast with 2 tablespoons (3T) of the water. Warm the honey and treacle very gently. Pour over the wheatgerm, add the remaining water and stir until the wheatgerm has dissolved.

Sift the flours, salt and spices into a warmed bowl. Make a well in the centre and pour in the yeast liquid, wheatgerm mixture and melted butter. With one hand or a spatula, gradually draw the flours into the liquid. Mix thoroughly until the dough comes cleanly away from the sides of the bowl. Add a little extra water if the dough seems too dry.

Turn onto a lightly floured board and knead for 10 minutes to form a smooth elastic ball. Place in a clean bowl, cover with a damp cloth and leave in a warm place for 1½-2 hours or until doubled in bulk.

Turn onto a floured surface and knead for 8 minutes. Shape into an oval loaf. Place on a baking sheet and put into an oiled polythene (plastic) bag. Leave in a warm place for 30-45 minutes or until doubled in bulk.
Brush with oil. Bake in the centre of a very hot oven, 475°F, Gas Mark 9 for 15 minutes. Lower the heat to 425°F, Gas Mark 8 and put the baking sheet on a lower shelf. Continue cooking for 20-30 minutes or until well browned. Cool on a wire rack.
Makes one 9 inch round loaf

French Bread

½ oz. (½ cake) fresh (compressed)
  yeast
½ pint + 4 tablespoons (1 ½ cups
  + 1T) warm water

1 lb. (4 cups) strong plain
  (all-purpose) flour
1 ¼ teaspoons salt

Cream the yeast with 2 tablespoons (3T) of the water. Sift the flour and salt into a warmed bowl and make a well in the centre. Pour in the yeast liquid and remaining water. With one hand or a spatula, draw the flour into the liquid and beat for 5 minutes.

Cover and leave to rest for 5 minutes, then beat again for 3 minutes. Place the bowl in an oiled polythene (plastic) bag and leave in a warm place for 3 hours until well risen and spongy to the touch.

Punch down the dough and turn onto a lightly floured surface. Knead for 5 minutes. Place in a clean bowl, put into an oiled polythene (plastic) bag and leave in a warm place for 3 hours or until trebled in size.

Turn onto a floured surface and cut into 3 equal pieces with a sharp knife. To form the loaves, roll each piece to an oval, about 10 inches long, fold in half lengthwise and seal the edges lightly with water. Roll over so the seam is on top. Press into an oval shape and fold in half again, but this time roll over so the seam is underneath. Roll into a 16 inch long sausage shape.

Place on a greased baking sheet and put inside an oiled polythene (plastic) bag. Leave in a warm place for 1½-2 hours until risen to 3 times the size. Remove from the bag.

Make 3 slashes on the top of each loaf and bake in a hot oven, 425°F, Gas Mark 7 for 30 minutes until golden brown. Cool on a wire rack.
Makes three French loaves

Bridge Rolls

½ oz. (½ cake) fresh (compressed)
  yeast
½ pint (1 ¼ cups) warm milk
1 lb. (4 cups) strong plain
  (all-purpose) flour

1 teaspoon salt
4 oz. (½ cup) butter
2 eggs, beaten
beaten egg to glaze

Blend yeast with 3 tablespoons (¼ cup) of the milk. Sift flour and salt into a bowl. Rub in the butter. Make a well in the centre and pour in the yeast liquid, eggs and remaining milk. Draw the dry ingredients into the liquid and mix until the dough comes away from the sides of the bowl.

Turn onto a floured surface and knead for 5-7 minutes. Put into a bowl, cover and leave in a warm place for 1½ hours until doubled in size.

Turn onto a floured surface and knead lightly for 3 minutes. Shape into finger rolls, about 3 inches long. Alternatively break the dough into small pieces and roll into balls. Arrange these in rows on a greased baking sheet, close together but not quite touching. Put into an oiled polythene (plastic) bag and leave in a warm place for 20-30 minutes until risen and touching. Remove from the bag and brush with the glaze. Bake in a hot oven, 425°F, Gas Mark 7 for 15 minutes. Cool on a wire tray.

Makes about 36 rolls

Biscottes

1 ½ oz. (1 ½ cakes) fresh
  (compressed) yeast
1 ½ pints (3 ¾ cups) warm milk
2 lb. (8 cups) strong plain
  (all-purpose) flour

6 oz. (¾ cup) butter
4 oz. (½ cup) castor (superfine)
  sugar
2 eggs
beaten egg to glaze

Cream the yeast with 2 tablespoons (3T) of the milk. Sift the flour into a bowl and make a well in the centre. Pour in the yeast together with half of the remaining milk. Draw enough of the flour into the liquid to make a thick batter. Sprinkle with flour and leave in a warm place for 20 minutes.

Cream the butter and sugar together until light and fluffy. Beat in the eggs. Add this creamed mixture, together with the remaining milk to the flour mixture and beat to form a smooth, elastic dough.

Turn onto a lightly floured surface and knead well. Cover with a damp cloth and leave in a warm place for 2 hours or until trebled in bulk.

Turn onto a floured surface and knead for 5 minutes. Shape into long, fat rolls. Place on a greased baking sheet and brush with egg glaze. Leave covered in a warm place for 10 minutes. Bake in a moderately hot oven, 400°F, Gas Mark 6 for 20-25 minutes. Cool on a wire rack.

The following day, cut into slices, ⅓ inch thick and bake in a cool oven, 325°F, Gas Mark 2 for 20 minutes, turn and bake for a further 10 minutes, until browned. Cool on a wire tray. Serve the biscottes cold.

Makes about 50 biscottes

BRIDGE ROLLS *(Photograph: Lintas London)*

Poppy Seed Bread

¾ oz. (¾ cake) fresh (compressed)
  yeast
¾ pint + 1 ½ tablespoons (2 cups)
  warm milk
2 lb. (8 cups) strong plain
  (all-purpose) flour

1 teaspoon salt
4 oz. (½ cup) butter
Glaze:
1 egg
1 tablespoon milk
2 tablespoons (3T) poppy seeds

Cream the yeast with 3 tablespoons (¼ cup) of the milk. Sift the flour and salt into a warmed bowl and rub in the butter. Make a well in the centre and pour in the yeast liquid and remaining milk. With one hand or a spatula, draw the ingredients together and continue to mix until the dough comes cleanly away from the sides of the bowl.

Turn onto a lightly floured surface and knead for 10 minutes until the dough is smooth and elastic. Place in a bowl, cover with a damp cloth and leave in a warm place for 1½ hours or until doubled in bulk.

Turn onto a floured surface and knead for 8 minutes. Roll the dough into an oblong, about 14 × 5 inches. With a sharp knife, cut into 3 strips lengthwise, leaving the dough joined at one end. Plait the strands to form a loaf. Moisten the ends with water and press them together.

Carefully lift onto a greased baking sheet, place in an oiled polythene (plastic) bag and leave in a warm place for 1 hour or until doubled in size. Remove from the bag.

For the glaze beat the egg with the milk. Brush the loaf with the glaze and sprinkle with the poppy seeds. Bake in a hot oven, 425°F, Gas Mark 7 for 45 minutes. Cool on a wire rack.

Makes one 2 lb. loaf

Note: If preferred, the loaf may be brushed with salted water instead of beaten egg and milk to glaze.

Rye Bread

½ oz. (½ cake) fresh (compressed) yeast
¾ pint (2 cups) warm water
1 lb. (4 cups) rye flour
8 oz. (2 cups) strong plain (all-purpose) flour
1 teaspoon salt
1 oz. (2T) castor (superfine) sugar

Cream the yeast with 3 tablespoons (¼ cup) of the water. Sift the flours and salt into a warmed bowl. Stir in the sugar. Make a well in the centre and pour in the yeast liquid and remaining water. Draw the flours into the liquid and mix until the dough comes cleanly away from the sides of the bowl.

Turn onto a floured surface and knead for 8-10 minutes until the dough is smooth and no longer sticky. Place in a bowl, cover with a damp cloth and leave in a warm place for 2-2½ hours until doubled in bulk.

Turn onto a floured surface and knead for a further 10 minutes. Divide the dough in half. Form each piece into a smooth ball and place on a greased baking sheet. Put into an oiled polythene (plastic) bag and leave in a warm place for 45 minutes or until doubled in size. Remove from the bag.

Bake in a moderately hot oven, 375°F, Gas Mark 5 for 45 minutes until golden brown. Turn onto a wire rack to cool.
Makes two 8 inch round loaves

Corn Bread

9 oz. (1 ¾ cups) ground yellow cornmeal
1 ¼ teaspoons salt
1 teaspoon castor (superfine) sugar
¼ pint + 4 tablespoons (1 cup) boiling water
2 ½ teaspoons oil
½ oz. (½ cake) fresh (compressed) yeast
3 tablespoons (¼ cup) warm water
8 oz. (2 cups) strong plain (all-purpose) flour

Put 6 oz. (1 ¼ cups) cornmeal, the salt, sugar and boiling water into a large bowl and beat until smooth. Stir in the oil and leave until lukewarm.

Cream the yeast with the warm water then stir into the cornmeal. Stir in 4 oz. (1 cup) flour. Beat thoroughly for 3 minutes, then cover and leave in a warm place for 30 minutes until doubled in bulk.

Turn onto a lightly floured surface and knead in the remaining flour. Continue kneading for 4 minutes. Form into a large round and place in a greased 9 inch round cake tin. Put into an oiled polythene (plastic) bag and leave in a warm place for 30 minutes until doubled in bulk. Remove from the bag.

Bake in a moderate oven, 350°F, Gas Mark 4 for 40 minutes until golden.
Makes one 9 inch round loaf

TRADITIONAL BREADS

Malt Loaf

1 oz. (1 cake) fresh (compressed)
 yeast
¼ pint + 4 tablespoons (1 cup)
 warm water
3 tablespoons (¼ cup) malt extract
2 tablespoons (3T) black treacle
 (molasses)

1 oz. (2T) butter, melted
1 lb. (4 cups) strong plain
 (all-purpose) flour
1 teaspoon salt
8 oz. (1⅓ cups) sultanas or
 seedless raisins

Blend the yeast with 3 tablespoons (¼ cup) of the water. Warm the malt extract and treacle over low heat. Stir in the remaining water, yeast liquid and butter.

Sift flour and salt into a warmed bowl, make a well in the centre and pour in the malt mixture. Draw the ingredients together. Mix in the fruit and beat until the dough comes cleanly away from the sides of the bowl.

Turn onto a floured surface and knead until the dough is smooth and elastic. Put into a lightly greased bowl, cover with a damp cloth and leave in a warm place for 1½-2 hours until doubled in bulk.

Knead gently for 4 minutes then divide the dough in half. Shape each piece into a loaf and place in a greased 1 lb. loaf tin. Put into an oiled polythene (plastic) bag and leave in a warm place for 45 minutes until risen to the top of the tins. Remove from the bag.

Bake in a hot oven, 450°F, Gas Mark 8 for 30-40 minutes until the loaves are browned and sound hollow when tapped underneath. Turn out and cool on a wire rack. When cold, wrap in foil. Serve the following day, sliced and buttered.

Makes two 1 lb. loaves

Barm Brack

½ oz. (½ cake) fresh (compressed)
  yeast
½ pint (1 ¼ cups) warm milk
1 lb. (4 cups) strong plain
  (all-purpose) flour
½ teaspoon salt
½ teaspoon ground cinnamon
1 teaspoon grated nutmeg
4 oz. (½ cup) castor (superfine)
  sugar
2 oz. (¼ cup) butter

2 eggs, lightly beaten
6 oz. (1 cup) sultanas (seedless
  white raisins)
6 oz. (1 cup) currants
4 oz. (⅔ cups) mixed (candied)
  peel, chopped
Glaze:
2 tablespoons (3T) castor
  (superfine) sugar
3 tablespoons (¼ cup) boiling
  water

Cream the yeast with 3 tablespoons (¼ cup) of the milk. Sift the flour, salt and spices into a warmed bowl. Stir in the sugar and rub in the butter. Make a well in the centre and pour in the yeast liquid, remaining milk and the eggs. With one hand or a spatula, draw all the ingredients together and beat until the dough is smooth and comes cleanly away from the sides of the bowl.

Turn onto a lightly floured board and knead in the dried fruit and peel. Continue kneading for 5 minutes or until the fruit is evenly incorporated and the dough is elastic in texture. Place in a clean bowl, cover with a damp cloth and leave in a warm place for 1½ hours or until doubled in bulk.

Turn onto a floured surface and knead lightly for 3 minutes. Divide the dough in half and shape each piece into a loaf. Place in greased 1 lb. loaf tins. Place the tins inside an oiled polythene (plastic) bag and leave in a warm place for 30 minutes until risen almost to the top of the tins. Remove from the bag.

Bake in a moderately hot oven, 400°F, Gas Mark 6 for 50-60 minutes. Make the glaze by dissolving the sugar in the water over moderate heat. Brush the tops of the loaves with the glaze 2-3 minutes before the end of the cooking time. Turn out and cool on a wire rack.
Makes two 1 lb. loaves

Date and Walnut Loaf

1 oz. (1 cake) fresh (compressed)
  yeast
½ pint (1 ¼ cups) warm water
2 tablespoons (3T) black treacle
  (molasses)
2 oz. (¼ cup) butter, melted

1 lb. (4 cups) wholemeal
  (wholewheat) flour
1 teaspoon salt
2 oz. (¼ cup) stoned (pitted)
  dates, chopped
2 oz. (½ cup) walnuts, chopped

Cream the yeast with 4 tablespoons (⅓ cup) water. Heat remaining water to boiling then add the treacle and butter. Cool until lukewarm.

Place the flour and salt in a warmed mixing bowl. Make a well in the centre and pour in the treacle mixture, yeast liquid, dates and walnuts. With a wooden spoon, draw the ingredients together and beat to form a smooth, soft dough. Continue to beat for 3-4 minutes. Cover with a damp cloth and leave to rise in a warm place for 1 hour or until doubled in size.

Turn onto a well floured board and knead for 4 minutes. Divide in half, form each piece into a loaf shape and place in greased 1 lb. loaf tins. Put the tins in an oiled polythene (plastic) bag and leave to rise in a warm place for 20 minutes. Remove from bag. Bake in a hot oven, 425°F, Gas Mark 7 for 35-40 minutes. Turn onto a wire tray to cool.

Makes two 1 lb. loaves

Sally Lunn

½ oz. (½ cake) fresh (compressed)
  yeast
2 tablespoons (3T) warm water
2 oz. (¼ cup) butter
¼ pint + 4 tablespoons (1 cup)
  milk
1 teaspoon sugar

1 egg, lightly beaten
1 lb. (4 cups) strong plain
  (all-purpose) flour
½ teaspoon salt
Glaze:
1 tablespoon sugar
1 tablespoon milk

Blend the yeast with the water. Melt the butter in a pan over low heat, then add the milk and sugar. Cool until lukewarm. Beat in the egg and yeast.

Sift flour and salt into a warmed bowl. Make a well in the centre and pour in the milk mixture. Draw flour into liquid and beat thoroughly.

Turn onto a lightly floured surface and knead for 10 minutes until smooth and elastic. Place in a clean bowl, cover with a damp cloth and leave in a warm place for 1½ hours or until doubled in size.

Turn onto a floured surface and knead lightly for 5 minutes. Shape into a 9 inch round and place on a greased baking sheet. Put inside an oiled polythene (plastic) bag and leave in a warm place for 40 minutes or until doubled in size. Remove from the bag.

Bake in a hot oven, 450°F, Gas Mark 8 for 20-25 minutes. For the glaze, dissolve the sugar in the milk over low heat. Brush over the loaf and return to the oven for 5 minutes. Turn onto a wire rack to cool.

Makes one 9 inch round loaf

Raisin Bread

12 oz. (2 cups) raisins
5 tablespoons (6T) sweet white
  wine
¾ oz. (¾ cake) fresh (compressed)
  yeast
¾ pint (2 cups) warm milk
6 oz. (¾ cup) butter, melted
3 oz. (¼ cup) black treacle
  (molasses)

6 oz. (1 cup) soft (light) brown
  sugar
1 lb. (4 cups) stoneground
  wholemeal (wholewheat) flour
1 lb. (4 cups) stoneground rye
  flour
1½ teaspoons salt

Simmer the raisins in the wine for 20 minutes. Drain, reserving
2 tablespoons (3T) of the wine. Cream the yeast with the reserved wine.
Pour the milk and butter over the treacle and mix thoroughly. Stir in the
brown sugar.

Place the flours and salt in a warmed bowl and mix well. Make a well in
the centre and add the yeast, milk mixture and raisins. With one hand or a
spatula, draw the flours into the liquid and beat until the dough comes
cleanly away from the sides of the bowl.

Turn onto a floured surface and knead for 8-10 minutes until the dough
is elastic and smooth. Place in a clean bowl and cover with a damp cloth.
Leave in a warm place for 1½-2 hours until doubled in bulk.

Knead thoroughly on a floured surface for 3-4 minutes. Divide the
dough in half and shape each piece into a loaf. Place in greased 1 lb. loaf
tins. Put the tins into an oiled polythene (plastic) bag and set aside in a
warm place for 30-40 minutes or until the dough has risen slightly.
Remove from the bag.

Bake in a very hot oven, 475°F, Gas Mark 9 for 15 minutes, then lower
the temperature to 425°F, Gas Mark 7 and put the tins on a low shelf.
Continue to cook for a further 25-30 minutes.

Turn out onto a wire rack to cool. Serve warm, sliced and buttered.
Makes two 1 lb. loaves

Lardy Cake

½ oz. (½ cake) fresh (compressed)
  yeast
½ pint (1¼ cups) warm milk
1 lb. (4 cups) strong plain
  (all-purpose) flour
1 teaspoon salt
4 oz. (½ cup) lard (shortening), cut
  into pieces
2 oz. (¼ cup) castor (superfine)
  sugar

1½ oz. (¼ cup) currants
1½ oz. (¼ cup) sultanas (seedless
  white raisins)
1 teaspoon mixed spice
Glaze:
3 tablespoons (¼ cup) sugar
3 tablespoons (¼ cup) water

Cream the yeast with 2 tablespoons (3T) of the milk. Sift the flour and salt into a bowl. Make a well in the centre and pour in the yeast liquid and remaining milk. Draw all the ingredients together with one hand or a spatula. Beat until the dough leaves the sides of the bowl clean.

Turn onto a floured surface and knead well for 5 minutes. Put into a clean bowl, cover with a damp cloth and leave in a warm place for 1½ hours.

Transfer to a floured surface and knead for 3 minutes, then shape into an oblong and roll out to ¼ inch thickness. Dot one-third of the lard over the dough to within ½ inch of the edges. Mix the sugar, dried fruit and spice together. Sprinkle one-third over the dough. Fold into 3, seal edges with a rolling pin and give the dough a half turn. Roll out into an oblong and cover with another third of the lard and fruit mixture. Fold, turn, roll and repeat with the remaining lard and fruit mixture.

Shape into a round, about 8 inches in diameter and place on a greased baking sheet. With the point of a sharp knife, score a diagonal pattern across the top. Put into an oiled polythene (plastic) bag and leave in a warm place for 30 minutes.

Remove from the bag and bake in a moderately hot oven, 400°F, Gas Mark 6 for 30 minutes. To make the glaze, dissolve the sugar in the water over moderate heat. Brush over the yeast cake and bake for a further 10 minutes. Cool on a wire rack for 5 minutes before serving.
Makes one 8 inch round yeast cake

Yorkshire Spice Bread

½ oz. (½ cake) fresh (compressed) yeast
½ pint (1 ¼ cups) warm milk
1 tablespoon golden (maple) syrup
1 lb. (4 cups) strong plain (all-purpose) flour
¼ teaspoon salt
4 oz. (½ cup) butter
4 oz. (½ cup) lard (shortening)
4 oz. (½ cup) castor (superfine) sugar

1 egg, beaten
2 oz. (⅓ cup) sultanas (seedless white raisins)
4 oz. (⅔ cup) currants
1 oz. (3T) mixed (candied) peel, chopped
1 teaspoon grated nutmeg
1 teaspoon ground cinnamon
Glaze:
2 tablespoons (3T) sugar
2 tablespoons (3T) water

Cream the yeast with 2 tablespoons (3T) of the milk. Dissolve the syrup in the remaining milk. Sift the flour and salt into a warmed bowl. Rub in the butter and lard. Stir in the sugar. Form a well in the centre of the dry ingredients and pour in the yeast, egg and milk mixture. With one hand or a spatula, draw the dry ingredients into the liquid and continue mixing until the dough comes cleanly away from the sides of the bowl.

Turn onto a floured surface and knead for 5 minutes. Put into a clean bowl, cover with a damp cloth and leave in a warm place for 1-1½ hours until doubled in size.

Turn onto a floured surface and knead in the dried fruit, peel and spices until evenly distributed and the dough is smooth. Divide in half and shape each piece into a loaf. Place in greased 1 lb. loaf tins. Put into oiled polythene (plastic) bags and leave in a warm place until risen almost to the top of the tins, about 25-30 minutes.

Bake in a hot oven, 450°F, Gas Mark 8 for 10 minutes, then reduce the temperature to moderate, 350°F, Gas Mark 4 and bake for a further 50 minutes.

For the glaze, dissolve the sugar in the water over moderate heat. Turn the loaves out onto a wire rack, brush with the sugar glaze and allow to cool.
Makes two 1 lb. loaves

Easter Bread

½ oz. (½ cake) fresh (compressed)
  yeast
½ pint (1¼ cups) warm milk
12 oz. (3 cups) strong plain
  (all-purpose) flour
½ teaspoon salt
1 teaspoon mixed spice
3 oz. (½ cup) seedless raisins
3 oz. (½ cup) sultanas (seedless
  white raisins)
1 oz. (3T) mixed (candied) peel,
  chopped
1 oz. (2T) butter, melted

Almond Paste:
3 oz. (¾ cup) ground almonds
1½ oz. (⅓ cup) icing
  (confectioners') sugar
1½ oz. (3T) castor (superfine)
  sugar
½ teaspoon lemon juice
few drops of almond essence
½ egg, beaten

milk for brushing
icing (confectioners') sugar for
  dusting

Cream the yeast with 3 tablespoons (¼ cup) of the milk. Sift the flour, salt and spice into a warmed bowl and make a well in the centre. Pour in the yeast liquid and the remaining milk. With one hand or a spatula, draw all the ingredients together and beat to give a soft dough.

Turn onto a lightly floured surface and knead for 4 minutes until the dough is smooth and elastic. Place in a clean bowl, cover with a damp cloth and leave in a warm place for 30 minutes or until well risen.

Knead the dough and work in the dried fruit, peel and butter. Turn onto a lightly floured surface and knead for 3 minutes. Form into an oblong, the same length as a 2 lb. loaf tin.

Work all the ingredients for the almond paste together. Form into a sausage shape and place on top of the dough. Mould the dough around the paste, tucking the join underneath. Place in a lined and greased 2 lb. loaf tin. Put into an oiled polythene (plastic) bag and leave in a warm place for 1 hour or until doubled in size. Remove from the bag and brush with a little milk.

Bake in a hot oven, 425°F, Gas Mark 7 for 10 minutes. Reduce the heat to moderate, 350°F, Gas Mark 4 and continue to bake for a further 45 minutes until evenly browned.

Turn onto a wire rack to cool, then dredge with icing sugar before serving, sliced and buttered.
Makes one 2 lb. loaf

EASTER BREAD *(Photograph: Dutch Dairy Bureau)*

Selkirk Bannock

½ oz. (½ cake) fresh (compressed)
  yeast
3 tablespoons (¼ cup) water
1 lb. (4 cups) strong plain
  (all-purpose) flour, sifted
8 oz. (2 cups) wholemeal
  (wholewheat) flour
1½ teaspoons salt
¾ pint (2 cups) warm milk
1 egg, beaten

4 oz. (½ cup) butter, softened
4 oz. (½ cup) lard (shortening),
  softened
4 oz. (⅔ cup) soft (light) brown
  sugar
8 oz. (1⅓ cups) sultanas (seedless
  white raisins)
4 oz. (⅔ cup) currants
4 oz. (⅔ cup) mixed (candied)
  peel, chopped

Cream the yeast with the water. Place the flours and salt in a warmed bowl. Make a well in the centre and pour in the yeast liquid, milk and beaten egg. With one hand or a spatula, gradually draw all the ingredients together and beat for 5 minutes.

Cover the bowl with a damp cloth and leave in a warm place for 1½ hours or until doubled in bulk. With a wooden spoon, beat in the softened butter and lard until the ingredients are thoroughly blended.

Turn onto a floured surface and pull out to a large square. Sprinkle the brown sugar, dried fruit and peel over the dough. Fold to enclose the filling and knead well for 5 minutes until the fruit is evenly distributed and the dough is smooth and elastic.

Divide in half and shape each piece into a loaf. Place in greased 1 lb. loaf tins. Put into an oiled polythene (plastic) bag and leave in a warm place for 30 minutes until risen to the top of the tins. Remove from the bag.

Bake in a moderately hot oven, 400°F, Gas Mark 6 for 50-60 minutes or until a skewer, inserted into the centre of the loaves, comes out clean. Leave in the tins for 10 minutes before turning out onto a wire rack to cool. Serve sliced, spread with butter.

Makes two 1 lb. loaves

Cornish Saffron Cake

1 teaspoon saffron strands
3 tablespoons (¼ cup) warm
  water
1 oz. (1 cake) fresh (compressed)
  yeast, crumbled
2 lb. (8 cups) strong plain
  (all-purpose) flour
8 oz. (1 cup) castor (superfine)
  sugar

½ pint (1¼ cups) warm milk
1 teaspoon salt
½ teaspoon grated nutmeg
½ teaspoon ground cinnamon
6 oz. (¾ cup) lard (shortening)
6 oz. (¾ cup) butter
8 oz. (1⅓ cups) mixed dried fruit
2 oz. (⅓ cup) lemon peel,
  chopped

Place the saffron and warm water in a small bowl and leave overnight. Blend yeast with 2 oz. (½ cup) of the flour, 1 teaspoon sugar and the milk. Leave in a warm place for 30 minutes until frothy. Strain the saffron strands, reserving the liquor.

Sift remaining flour, salt and spices into a warmed bowl and stir in the remaining sugar. Rub in the lard and butter. Make a well in the centre and pour in the yeast batter and saffron liquor. Draw the ingredients together and beat to give a soft dough.

Turn onto a floured surface and knead for 5 minutes. Put into a clean bowl, cover with a damp cloth and leave in a warm place for 1½-2 hours until doubled in bulk.

Turn onto a floured surface and knead in the fruit and peel. Divide in half and shape into two loaves. Place in greased 1 lb. loaf tins. Put into oiled polythene (plastic) bags and leave for 30 minutes or until well risen. Remove from the bags.

Bake in a hot oven, 425°F, Gas Mark 7 for 40 minutes. Turn out and cool on a wire tray.

Makes two 1 lb. loaves

TRADITIONAL BUNS, TEACAKES AND ROLLS

Devonshire Splits

½ oz. (½ cake) fresh (compressed)
  yeast
½ pint (1¼ cups) warm milk
1 lb. (4 cups) strong plain
  (all-purpose) flour
½ teaspoon salt

½ teaspoon ground cinnamon
3 oz. (⅓ cup) castor (superfine)
  sugar
2 oz. (¼ cup) butter
jam and whipped or clotted cream
  for filling

Cream the yeast with 3 tablespoons (¼ cup) of the milk. Sift flour, salt and
cinnamon into a warmed bowl. Stir in the sugar and rub in the butter.
Make a well in the centre and pour in the yeast liquid. Draw the ingredients
together and beat to a smooth dough, adding more milk if required.

Knead on a lightly floured surface for 4 minutes. Place in a bowl, cover
with a damp cloth and leave in a warm place until doubled in size.

Turn onto a floured surface and knead lightly. Divide the dough into
14-16 pieces. Roll each into a ball, place well apart on a greased baking
sheet and flatten the tops slightly. Place in an oiled polythene (plastic) bag
and leave in a warm place for 30 minutes. Remove from the bag. Bake in a
hot oven, 425°F, Gas Mark 7 for 15 minutes. Cool on a wire rack.

Before serving, split the buns and spread with jam and cream.

Makes 14-16 buns

Muffins

½ oz. (½ cake) fresh (compressed)
  yeast
4 tablespoons (⅓ cup) warm
  water
½ pint (1¼ cups) warm milk

1 egg, beaten
1 oz. (2T) butter, melted
1 lb. (4 cups) strong plain
  (all-purpose) flour
½ teaspoon salt

Cream the yeast with the water. Combine the milk, egg and butter. Sift
flour and salt into a warmed bowl and make a well in the centre. Pour in the
yeast liquid and milk mixture. Beat until smooth.

Turn onto a floured surface and knead for 8 minutes to give a soft,
elastic dough. Put into a clean bowl, cover with a damp cloth and leave in a
warm place for 1½ hours or until doubled in size.

On a floured surface, roll the dough to ½ inch thickness. Cut out rounds,
using a 2½ inch plain pastry cutter. Grease a griddle or heavy frying pan
(skillet) and place over a low heat. Cook the muffins on both sides until
lightly browned. Serve toasted on both sides, split and buttered.

Makes about 12 muffins

Chelsea Buns

1 oz. (1 cake) fresh (compressed)
  yeast
5 oz. (⅔ cup) castor (superfine)
  sugar
¼ pint (⅔ cup) warm milk
1 lb. (4 cups) strong plain
  (all-purpose) flour
1 teaspoon salt
2 eggs, lightly beaten

4 oz. (½ cup) butter, melted
2 oz. (⅓ cup) currants
2 oz. (⅓ cup) sultanas (seedless
  white raisins)
1 oz. (3T) mixed (candied) peel,
  chopped
1 tablespoon grated orange rind
1 teaspoon mixed spice

Cream the yeast with 1 teaspoon of the sugar, the milk and 4 oz. (1 cup) of the flour. Leave in a warm place for 15-20 minutes until frothy.

Sift the remaining flour and the salt into a warmed bowl and stir in 2 oz. (¼ cup) of the sugar. Make a well in the centre and pour in the yeast batter, beaten eggs and the melted butter. With one hand or a spatula, draw the flour into the liquid and beat until the dough comes cleanly away from the sides of the bowl.

Turn onto a lightly floured surface and knead for 5 minutes. Place in a clean bowl, cover with a damp cloth and leave in a warm place for 1½ hours or until doubled in size. Mix together 2 oz. (¼ cup) sugar, the currants, sultanas, peel, orange rind and mixed spice.

Knead the dough again for 5 minutes. Divide in half and roll each piece of dough to a rectangle. Sprinkle with the fruit mixture. Roll up as for a Swiss (jelly) roll. With a sharp knife, cut into slices, about 1½ inches thick.

Place the slices, cut side down, close together, but not quite touching, on a baking sheet. Put into an oiled polythene (plastic) bag and leave in a warm place for 30 minutes until risen and touching. Remove from the bag.

Dissolve the remaining 1 oz. (2T) of sugar in a little warm water to form a thin glaze. Brush the buns with the glaze and bake in a moderately hot oven, 375°F, Gas Mark 5 for 30-35 minutes.

Turn onto a wire rack and allow to cool slightly before pulling apart.
Makes about 18 buns

Swiss Buns

½ oz. (½ cake) fresh (compressed)
  yeast
1 teaspoon castor (superfine)
  sugar
¼ pint + 2 tablespoons (¾ cup)
  warm milk
12 oz. (3 cups) strong plain
  (all-purpose) flour

½ teaspoon salt
1 oz. (2T) margarine
1 egg, beaten
beaten egg to glaze
Glacé icing:
4 oz. (1 cup) icing (confectioners')
  sugar
2-3 teaspoons hot water

Blend the yeast with the sugar, milk and 3 oz. (¾ cup) of the flour. Leave
in a warm place for 15-20 minutes until frothy.

Sift remaining flour and salt into a bowl and rub in the margarine. Make
a well in the centre and stir in the yeast batter and beaten egg. Draw the
ingredients together and mix to a fairly stiff dough.

Turn onto a floured surface and knead for 5 minutes. Place in a lightly
greased bowl and cover with a damp cloth. Leave in a warm place for
1½ hours or until doubled in size.

Turn onto a floured surface and knead for 3 minutes. Divide into
8 pieces and shape into 5 inch long rolls. Place, well apart, on a greased
baking sheet. Put inside an oiled polythene (plastic) bag and leave in a
warm place for 30 minutes until almost doubled in size. Remove from the
bag.

Brush the rolls with beaten egg. Bake in a hot oven, 425°F, Gas Mark 7
for 15-20 minutes until golden brown and well risen.

Turn onto a wire rack to cool. Blend the icing sugar with enough hot
water to give a smooth, coating consistency. When cold, decorate the buns
with the glacé icing.
Makes 8 buns

Baps

½ oz. (½ cake) fresh (compressed)
  yeast
½ pint (1¼ cups) warm milk and
  water, mixed
1 lb. (4 cups) strong plain
  (all-purpose) flour

1 teaspoon salt
2 oz. (¼ cup) lard (shortening)
flour for dusting

Cream the yeast with 3 tablespoons (¼ cup) of the liquid. Sift flour and salt into a bowl. Rub in the lard. Make a well in the centre and pour in the yeast and remaining liquid. Work to a firm dough.

Knead on a lightly floured surface for 5 minutes. Place in a bowl, cover with a damp cloth and leave in a warm place for 1½ hours or until doubled in size.

Knead the dough lightly for 3 minutes, then divide into 8-10 pieces. Shape each into a ball and place, well apart, on a floured baking sheet. Flatten the baps and press the floured handle of a wooden spoon into the centre of each one. Put into an oiled polythene (plastic) bag and leave to rise in a warm place for 45 minutes or until doubled in size. Remove from the bag.

Dust lightly with flour and bake in a moderately hot oven, 400°F, Gas Mark 6 for 20-25 minutes until lightly browned. Cool on a wire rack.
Makes 8-10 baps

Crumpets

½ oz. (½ cake) fresh (compressed)
  yeast
1 pint (2½ cups) warm milk
1 lb. (4 cups) strong plain
  (all-purpose) flour

1 teaspoon salt
½ teaspoon bicarbonate of soda
  (baking soda)

Cream the yeast with 3 tablespoons (¼ cup) of the milk. Sift flour and salt into a warmed bowl and make a well in the centre. Pour in the yeast and remaining liquid. Beat well for 5 minutes then cover and leave in a warm place for 1 hour until risen.

Dissolve the bicarbonate of soda in a little warm water and pour onto the spongy batter. Beat for 3-4 minutes. Cover and leave in a warm place for 45 minutes.

Grease a griddle or heavy frying pan (skillet) and 6 crumpet rings or 3 inch plain metal cutters. Heat the griddle over a low to moderate heat. Pour about 2 tablespoonfuls (3T) of the batter into each ring and cook each crumpet until the top has set and the bottom is golden brown. Remove the rings, turn the crumpets and cook for 3 minutes.

Serve toasted on both sides and spread with butter.
Makes about 20 crumpets

Bath Buns

½ oz. (½ cake) fresh (compressed) yeast

3 oz. (⅓ cup) castor (superfine) sugar

¼ pint (⅔ cup) warm milk

4 tablespoons (⅓ cup) warm water

1 lb. (4 cups) strong plain (all-purpose) flour

½ teaspoon salt

2 oz. (¼ cup) butter

2 eggs, lightly beaten

4 oz. (⅔ cup) currants

2 oz. (⅓ cup) mixed (candied) peel

Glaze:

½ egg, beaten

1 tablespoon milk

2 tablespoons (3T) crushed lump sugar

Blend the yeast with 1 teaspoon of the sugar, the milk, water and 4 oz. (1 cup) of the flour. Leave in a warm place for about 20 minutes, until frothy.

Sift remaining flour and the salt into a warmed bowl and stir in the sugar. Rub in the butter. Make a well in the centre and pour in the yeast batter and beaten eggs. Mix thoroughly then knead lightly to yield a soft dough.

Put into a lightly greased bowl, cover with a damp cloth and leave in a warm place for 1 hour or until doubled in size.

Turn onto a floured board and knead in the currants and peel. Place 12 tablespoons of dough, well apart, on a greased baking sheet. Put into a polythene (plastic) bag and leave to rise in a warm place for 30 minutes. Remove from the bag.

Beat the egg with the milk and brush over the buns. Sprinkle with sugar. Bake in a moderately hot oven, 400°F, Gas Mark 6 for 20-25 minutes. Cool on a wire rack.

Makes 12 buns

Hot Cross Buns

1 oz. (1 cake) fresh (compressed)
  yeast
¼ pint (⅔ cup) warm milk
4 tablespoons (⅓ cup) warm
  water
2 oz. (¼ cup) castor (superfine)
  sugar
1 lb. (4 cups) strong plain
  (all-purpose) flour
1 teaspoon salt
2 teaspoons mixed spice
2 oz. (¼ cup) margarine

1 oz. (3T) currants
2 oz. (⅓ cup) sultanas (seedless
  white raisins)
1 oz. (3T) mixed (candied) peel,
  chopped
1 egg, beaten
Glaze:
1 tablespoon castor (superfine)
  sugar
1 tablespoon milk
1 tablespoon water

Blend the yeast with the milk, water, 1 teaspoon of the sugar and 4 oz. (1 cup) of the flour. Leave in a warm place for 15-20 minutes until frothy.

Sift the remaining flour, salt and mixed spice into a warmed bowl. Stir in the remaining sugar and rub in the margarine. Stir in the dried fruit and peel. Make a well in the centre and pour in the beaten egg and yeast batter. With one hand or a spatula, draw all the ingredients together and beat until the mixture comes cleanly away from the sides of the bowl.

Turn onto a lightly floured surface and knead well for 7 minutes. Place in a clean bowl, cover with a damp cloth and leave in a warm place for 1½ hours or until doubled in size.

Turn onto a lightly floured surface and knead for 3 minutes. Divide into 12 pieces and shape into buns. Place on a greased baking sheet. Put inside an oiled polythene (plastic) bag and leave in a warm place for 30 minutes until doubled in size. Remove from the bag.

Mark crosses on top of the buns with the point of a sharp knife. Bake in a moderately hot oven, 400°F, Gas Mark 6 for 15-20 minutes until golden brown.

To make the glaze, dissolve the sugar in the milk and water over moderate heat. Brush over the buns whilst still warm. Transfer to a wire rack to cool.

Makes 12 buns
Note: If preferred, strips of shortcrust pastry (basic pie dough) or sweet flan pastry may be used to make the crosses.

FANCY BREADS

Bran Teabread

1 oz. (1 cake) fresh (compressed)
  yeast
¼ pint (⅔ cup) warm water
3 oz. (1¼ cups) All-bran cereal
¼ pint (⅔ cup) warm milk
1 lb. (4 cups) strong plain
  (all-purpose) flour
1 teaspoon salt
1 oz. (2T) castor (superfine) sugar
grated rind of 1 orange
1 egg, beaten

Icing:
4 oz. (1 cup) icing (confectioners')
  sugar, sifted
1 tablespoon hot water
  (approximately)
Decoration:
glacé (candied) cherries, chopped
glacé (candied) pineapple,
  chopped
angelica, chopped

Cream the yeast with the water. Soak the bran in the milk for 10 minutes. Sift the flour and salt into a bowl and stir in the sugar and orange rind. Form a well in the centre and pour in the yeast liquid, beaten egg and the bran mixture. With one hand or a spatula, draw the ingredients together and beat until the dough comes cleanly away from the sides of the bowl.

Turn onto a lightly floured surface and knead for 5 minutes until the dough is smooth and firm. Place in a clean bowl, cover with a damp cloth and leave in a warm place for 1½ hours or until doubled in size.

Turn onto a lightly floured surface and knead for 1-2 minutes. Divide into 3 equal pieces. Roll each into a strand, about 15 inches long. Gather the ends together and plait the strands.

Place on a greased baking sheet, curving the plait to form a ring. Press the ends together firmly. Place in an oiled polythene (plastic) bag and leave to rise in a warm place for 15 minutes. Remove from the bag. Bake in a hot oven, 425°F, Gas Mark 7 for 15-20 minutes. Turn onto a wire rack and allow to cool.

To make the icing, blend the icing sugar with enough hot water to give a smooth coating consistency. Trickle over the bread and sprinkle with the glacé fruits and angelica.
Makes one tea ring

BRAN TEABREAD *(Photograph: Kelloggs Kitchen)*

Swiss Yeast Cake

¾ oz. (¾ cake) fresh (compressed)
  yeast
1 tablespoon warm water
1 ½ lb. (6 cups) strong plain
  (all-purpose) flour
1 teaspoon salt
4 oz. (½ cup) castor (superfine)
  sugar
¼ pint + 4 tablespoons (1 cup)
  warm milk
4 oz. (½ cup) butter, melted
2 egg yolks, lightly beaten

Filling:
3 egg whites
4 oz. (½ cup) castor (superfine)
  sugar
6 oz. (1 ½ cups) walnuts, finely
  chopped
grated rind of 1 orange
grated rind of 1 lemon
1 teaspoon grated nutmeg
Topping:
3 tablespoons (¼ cup) clear
  honey, warmed
12 walnut halves
crystallized (candied) orange and
  lemon slices

Cream the yeast with the water. Sift the flour and salt into a large bowl. Stir in the sugar and make a well in the centre. Pour in the milk, butter, egg yolks and the yeast liquid. With one hand or a spatula, draw the flour into the liquid and beat until the dough comes away from the sides of the bowl.

Turn onto a lightly floured surface and knead thoroughly for 8-10 minutes until smooth and elastic. Place in a clean bowl, cover with a damp cloth and leave to rise in a warm place for 1 ½ hours or until doubled in size.

Meanwhile make the filling. Whisk the egg whites until they form soft peaks. Fold in the sugar, a little at a time, using a metal spoon, then beat until smooth and glossy. Fold in the nuts, orange rind, lemon rind and nutmeg.

Turn the dough onto a floured surface and knead for 5 minutes. Cut the dough into 2 pieces and roll each to a large rectangle. Spread with the filling. Roll up each piece of dough as for a Swiss (jelly) roll. Place on separate greased baking sheets and form each roll into a circle, dampening the edges and pressing them together to seal.

Place in oiled polythene (plastic) bags and leave in a warm place for 45 minutes or until doubled in size. Remove from the bag. Bake in a hot oven, 425°F, Gas Mark 7 for 15 minutes. Reduce the temperature to moderate, 350°F, Gas Mark 4 and continue to bake for 40 minutes.

Turn onto a wire rack and cool for 15 minutes. Brush with honey. Decorate with walnut halves and crystallized (candied) fruit slices.
Makes two tea rings

Kugelhupf

½ oz. (½ cake) fresh (compressed)
 yeast
¼ pint + 4 tablespoons (1 cup)
 warm milk
8 oz. (1 cup) butter
6 oz. (¾ cup) castor (superfine)
 sugar
4 eggs

1 lb. (4 cups) strong plain
 (all-purpose) flour
¼ teaspoon salt
finely grated rind of 1 orange
6 oz. (1 cup) seedless raisins
2 oz. (½ cup) walnuts, chopped
icing (confectioners') sugar for
 dusting

Blend yeast with 4 tablespoons (⅓ cup) of the milk. Cream butter and
sugar together until light and fluffy. Beat in the eggs, one at a time. Stir in
the yeast liquid and half of the flour. Add remaining milk and beat well.
Fold in remaining flour, salt, orange rind, raisins and nuts.

Turn into a greased Kugelhupf mould or a large ring mould; the dough
should only half fill the tin. Put into an oiled polythene (plastic) bag and
leave in a warm place for 2 hours or until almost risen to the top of the tin.
Remove from the bag.

Bake in a moderate oven, 350°F, Gas Mark 4 for 40 minutes or until a
skewer, inserted into the centre of the cake, comes out clean.

Leave in the tin for 30 minutes before turning out onto a wire rack to
cool. Sprinkle with icing sugar before serving.
Makes one 9 inch round yeast cake

Egg and Brandy Cake

½ oz. (½ cake) fresh (compressed)
  yeast
2 tablespoons (3T) warm milk
1 lb. (4 cups) strong plain
  (all-purpose) flour
1 teaspoon salt
6 oz. (¾ cup) castor (superfine)
  sugar

4 eggs, beaten
1 oz. (2T) butter, melted
3 tablespoons (¼ cup) brandy
Glaze:
1 egg yolk
2 tablespoons (3T) milk
2 oz. (⅓ cup) soft (light) brown
  sugar

Cream the yeast with the milk. Sift the flour and salt into a warmed bowl. Stir in the sugar. Make a well in the centre. Pour in the eggs, butter, brandy and yeast liquid. With one hand or a wooden spoon, gradually draw the dry ingredients into the liquid and beat until a smooth dough is formed.

Turn onto a lightly floured surface and knead thoroughly for 5-7 minutes until smooth and elastic. Place in a clean bowl, cover and leave in a warm place for 2 hours or until risen to twice the size.

Turn onto a floured surface and knead lightly for 5 minutes. Shape into an 8 inch round. Put into a greased 8 inch cake tin and press to the sides. Beat the egg yolk with the milk and brush over the dough. Sprinkle with brown sugar. Put into an oiled polythene (plastic) bag and leave in a warm place for 20 minutes. Remove from the bag.

Bake in a hot oven, 425°F, Gas Mark 7 for 10 minutes then reduce the temperature to 375°F, Gas Mark 5 and bake for a further 55-60 minutes until golden brown.

Remove from the tin and cool on a wire tray. Serve cold, sliced and spread with butter.
Makes one 8 inch round yeast cake

EGG AND BRANDY CAKE (Photograph: Egg Marketing Board)

Alsace Loaf

4 oz. (⅔ cup) prunes
¼ pint (⅔ cup) orange juice
½ oz. (½ cake) fresh (compressed)
  yeast
½ teaspoon castor (superfine)
  sugar
¼ pint (⅔ cup) warm milk
4 oz. (1 cup) strong plain
  (all-purpose) flour

8 oz. (2 cups) wholemeal
  (wholewheat) flour
½ teaspoon salt
¼ teaspoon mixed spice
1 oz. (3T) soft (light) brown sugar
1 oz. (2T) butter
2 tablespoons (3T) clear honey,
  warmed

Soak the prunes in the orange juice overnight. Simmer in the soaking liquid until tender, then drain, reserving 3 tablespoons (¼ cup) of the orange juice. Stone the prunes.

Blend yeast with the reserved orange juice, castor sugar, milk and plain flour. Leave in a warm place for 15-20 minutes until frothy.

Place the wholemeal flour, salt and spice in a warmed bowl. Stir in the brown sugar and rub in the butter. Make a well in the centre and add the yeast batter. Mix well and beat until the dough comes cleanly away from the sides of the bowl.

Turn onto a floured surface and knead in the prunes. Continue to knead for 5 minutes. Shape into a loaf and place in a greased 1 lb. loaf tin. Put into an oiled polythene (plastic) bag and leave in a warm place for 1 hour or until doubled in size. Remove from the bag.

Bake in a hot oven, 450°F, Gas Mark 8 for 40-45 minutes until golden brown and hollow when tapped underneath. Leave in the tin for 10 minutes then turn out onto a wire rack. Brush with honey. Allow to cool before serving.

Makes one 1 lb. loaf

Genoese Bread

1 oz. (1 cake) fresh (compressed)
  yeast
6 oz. (¾ cup) castor (superfine)
  sugar
¾ pint (2 cups) warm milk
2 lb. (8 cups) strong plain
  (all-purpose) flour
1 teaspoon salt
2 tablespoons (3T) orange flower
  water
3 oz. (⅓ cup) butter, melted

6 oz. (1 cup) seedless raisins
3 tablespoons (¼ cup) Marsala
2 oz. (½ cup) pine nuts or
  almonds, chopped
2 oz. (½ cup) pistachio nuts
2 teaspoons fennel seeds, crushed
½ teaspoon aniseed, crushed
2 oz. (⅓ cup) mixed (candied)
  peel, chopped
1 tablespoon grated lemon rind
1 tablespoon grated orange rind

Blend the yeast with 1 teaspoon of the sugar, the milk and 10 oz.
(2½ cups) of the flour. Leave in a warm place for 15-20 minutes until
frothy.

Sift the remaining flour and the salt into a warmed bowl. Stir in the
remaining sugar. Make a well in the centre and pour in the orange flower
water, melted butter and the yeast mixture. With one hand or a spatula,
draw the dry ingredients into the centre and beat until the dough comes
cleanly away from the sides of the bowl.

Turn onto a lightly floured surface and knead for 8 minutes until the
dough is smooth and elastic. Place in a clean bowl, cover with a damp cloth
and leave in a warm place for 1½ hours or until doubled in bulk.

Meanwhile soak the raisins in the Marsala for 30 minutes then drain.
Turn the dough onto a floured surface and pull out to a square, about
½ inch thick. Sprinkle evenly with the nuts, raisins, fennel seeds, aniseed,
mixed peel, lemon and orange rind. Roll up as for a Swiss (jelly) roll.
Flatten to a square, approximately 1 inch thick. Roll up as before then
flatten to a 9 inch round and place on a greased baking sheet. Put into an
oiled polythene (plastic) bag and leave in a warm place for 1-1½ hours
until doubled in bulk.

Remove from the bag and, with the point of a sharp knife, make a
triangle on top of the dough. Bake in a moderately hot oven, 375°F, Gas
Mark 5 for 20 minutes, then reduce the temperature to moderate, 325°F,
Gas Mark 3 and bake for a further 45-55 minutes until firm and golden
brown.

Cool completely on a wire rack before serving with unsalted (sweet)
butter.

Makes one 9 inch round yeast cake

Stollen

¼ oz. (¼ cake) fresh (compressed) yeast
6 tablespoons (½ cup) warm milk
8 oz. (2 cups) strong plain (all-purpose) flour
½ teaspoon salt
2 oz. (¼ cup) butter
2 oz. (¼ cup) castor (superfine) sugar
1 egg, beaten
3 oz. (½ cup) seedless raisins
2 oz. (⅓ cup) currants or chopped glacé (candied) cherries
1 oz. (3T) mixed (candied) peel, chopped
1 oz. (¼ cup) blanched almonds, chopped
grated rind of ½ lemon
½ oz. (1T) butter, melted
icing (confectioners') sugar for dusting

Cream the yeast with 2 tablespoons (3T) of the milk. Sift the flour and salt into a warmed bowl. Make a well in the centre. Cream the butter with the sugar, add the egg and beat well. Add to the flour, with the remaining milk, yeast liquid, fruit, peel, nuts and lemon rind. With one hand or a spatula, draw the ingredients together and beat until the dough comes cleanly away from the sides of the bowl.

Turn onto a lightly floured surface and knead well for 5 minutes. Place in a clean bowl, cover with a damp cloth and leave in a warm place for 1½ hours or until doubled in size.

Turn onto a lightly floured surface and knead well for 5 minutes. Roll to an oblong, about 10 × 8 inches. Brush with melted butter. Fold over lengthwise so the top layer is 1 inch from the edge of the bottom, forming a split loaf shape.

Place on a greased baking sheet and put inside an oiled polythene (plastic) bag. Leave in a warm place for 30 minutes until doubled in size. Remove from the bag. Bake in a moderately hot oven, 375°F, Gas Mark 5 for 35-45 minutes until golden brown.

Turn onto a wire rack to cool. Sprinkle the top generously with icing sugar before serving.
Makes one 10 inch stollen

Apple Slice

½ oz. (½ cake) fresh (compressed)
  yeast
¼ pint (⅔ cup) warm milk
8 oz. (2 cups) strong plain
  (all-purpose) flour
½ teaspoon salt
2 oz. (¼ cup) castor (superfine)
  sugar
2 oz. (¼ cup) butter, melted
1 egg, beaten
Filling:
1 cooking apple, peeled, cored
  and grated
3 oz. (½ cup) seedless raisins,
  halved

1 oz. (3T) mixed (candied) peel,
  finely chopped
2 oz. (⅓ cup) demerara (raw)
  sugar
grated rind of ½ orange
½ teaspoon ground cinnamon
Glaze:
1 egg, beaten
Glacé Icing:
4 oz. (1 cup) icing (confectioners')
  sugar, sifted
2-3 teaspoons hot water

Cream the yeast with 2 tablespoons (3T) of the milk. Sift the flour and salt
into a bowl then stir in the sugar. Make a well in the centre of the dry
ingredients. Pour in the yeast liquid, remaining milk, butter and beaten
egg. With one hand or a wooden spoon, gradually draw all the ingredients
together and beat until the dough is smooth and leaves the sides of the
bowl clean.

Cover and leave in a warm place for 45 minutes until well risen and
puffy. Turn onto a floured board and knead for 5-7 minutes until the
dough is elastic and no longer sticky. Shape into an oblong and roll to a
strip 14 × 6 inches. Transfer to a large greased baking sheet.

Mix the filling ingredients together and place down the centre of the
dough. At each side of the filling, make 2 inch cuts diagonally with a sharp
knife at ¾ inch intervals. Fold the strips alternately over the filling. Seal the
edges with water.

Place in an oiled polythene (plastic) bag and leave to rise in a warm place
for 20-25 minutes until doubled in size. Remove from the bag. Brush with
beaten egg and bake in a moderately hot oven, 400°F, Gas Mark 6 for
30-35 minutes.

Turn onto a wire rack to cool. Blend the icing sugar with enough water to
give a thin coating consistency. Whilst still warm, brush the slice with glacé
icing. Serve cold, cut into slices.
Makes one 14 inch slice

Scottish Tart

½ oz. (½ cake) fresh (compressed)
  yeast
¼ pint (⅔ cup) warm milk
8 oz. (2 cups) plain (all-purpose)
  flour
1 teaspoon salt
1 small egg, beaten
1 oz. (2T) margarine, softened
Filling:
4 oz. marzipan
½ oz. (2T) blanched almonds,
  chopped
1½ oz. (4½T) mixed (candied)
  peel

1 oz. (3T) sultanas (seedless white
  raisins)
Custard:
2 tablespoons (3T) cornflour
  (cornstarch)
¾ pint (2 cups) milk
2 oz. (¼ cup) castor (superfine)
  sugar
few drops of vanilla essence
2 large eggs, beaten
Glaze:
beaten egg

Cream the yeast with 2 tablespoons (3T) of milk. Sift the flour and salt into a warmed bowl. Make a well in the centre and pour in the yeast liquid, remaining milk and the beaten egg. With one hand, gradually work the flour into the liquid to form a fairly stiff dough.

Turn onto a floured surface and knead for 5 minutes until smooth and elastic. Form into a round and put the softened margarine in the centre. Gather the dough over the margarine and knead until thoroughly incorporated. Put into an oiled polythene (plastic) bag and leave in a warm place for 45 minutes or until doubled in bulk.

Turn onto a lightly floured surface and knead lightly. Roll into a 10 inch circle and line an 8 inch flan ring, pressing the dough well into the sides and base. Trim off the surplus dough by rolling and keep the trimmings.

Roll the marzipan on a sugared surface to a 7 inch circle. Place on top of the dough round. Mix the almonds with the peel and dried fruit and scatter over the marzipan.

To make the custard, blend the cornflour with 3 tablespoons (¼ cup) of the milk and the sugar. Heat the remaining milk to boiling, then gradually pour onto the cornflour, stirring constantly. Return to the pan and bring to the boil, stirring. Cook, stirring, for 2 minutes until thickened. Add the vanilla essence. Pour onto the eggs, gradually, beating well. Return to the pan and heat gently, stirring, until the custard is smooth and creamy. Pour into the flan.

Roll out the scraps of dough and cut out 7 rounds using a 1½ inch plain pastry cutter. Arrange 6 around the edge of the flan and one in the centre. Brush with beaten egg. Place in an oiled polythene (plastic) bag and leave in a warm place for about 20 minutes. Bake in a moderate oven, 350°F, Gas Mark 4 for 30 minutes. Serve hot or cold.
Makes one 8 inch tart

Savarin

1 oz. (1 cake) fresh (compressed)
  yeast
6 tablespoons (½ cup) warm milk
1½ oz. (3T) castor sugar
8 oz. (2 cups) strong plain
  (all-purpose) flour
½ teaspoon salt
4 eggs, beaten
4 oz. (½ cup) butter, softened
Syrup:
1¼ lb. (2¼ cups) sugar
1 pint (2½ cups) water
6 tablespoons (½ cup) rum

Glaze:
3 tablespoons (¼ cup) apricot
  jam, sieved
1 tablespoon water
Filling:
8 oz. (1½ cups) strawberries,
  hulled and halved
4 oz. (1 cup) green grapes, halved
  and deseeded
2-3 slices fresh pineapple, cut into
  ½ inch cubes

Blend the yeast with the milk, 1 teaspoon of the sugar and 2 oz. (½ cup) of the flour. Leave in a warm place for 15-20 minutes until frothy.

Sift the remaining flour and salt into a warmed bowl and stir in the remaining sugar. Make a well in the centre and pour in the eggs and yeast mixture. Add the softened butter and gradually draw all the ingredients together. Beat thoroughly for 3-4 minutes.

Pour into a greased 9 inch savarin tin or ring mould and place inside an oiled polythene (plastic) bag. Leave in a warm place for 30-40 minutes or until the dough has risen to the top of the mould. Remove from the bag. Bake in a moderately hot oven, 400°F, Gas Mark 6 for 25 minutes or until golden brown.

Meanwhile, prepare the syrup by dissolving the sugar in the water in a heavy saucepan over a gentle heat. When dissolved, bring to the boil and boil for 1 minute. Remove from the heat and stir in the rum.

Turn the savarin out onto a wire rack, placed over a plate. Allow to cool for a few minutes then make holes over the surface with a fine skewer. Set aside ¼ pint (⅔ cup) of the syrup. Spoon the rest of the syrup over the savarin until it has soaked through. Leave to cool then transfer to a serving dish.

Warm the apricot jam with the water and brush over the savarin. Mix the fruit with the reserved syrup and pile into the centre. Serve with cream.
Makes one 9 inch savarin

SAVARIN *(Photograph: Flour Advisory Bureau)*

Bavarian Nut Pastry Roll

½ oz. (½ cake) fresh (compressed)
  yeast
2 oz. (¼ cup) castor (superfine)
  sugar
¼ pint + 2 tablespoons (¾ cup)
  warm milk
1 lb. (4 cups) plain (all-purpose)
  flour
1 teaspoon salt
1 teaspoon ground cinnamon
10 oz. (1¼ cups) butter
2 eggs, lightly beaten
Filling:
12 oz. (3 cups) hazelnuts (filberts),
  chopped
4 oz. (1 cup) blanched almonds,
  chopped

4 oz. (⅔ cup) soft (light) brown
  sugar
2 tablespoons (3T) glacé
  (candied) cherries, chopped
1 tablespoon chopped angelica
3-4 dried apricots, soaked,
  drained and chopped
grated rind of 1 lemon
½ teaspoon ground cinnamon
¼ teaspoon mixed spice
2 tablespoons (3T) double
  (heavy) cream
6 tablespoons (½ cup) clear
  honey, warmed
3 tablespoons (¼ cup) dark rum
Glaze:
1 egg, lightly beaten

Blend the yeast with 1 teaspoon of the sugar, the milk and 5 oz. (1¼ cups) of the flour. Leave in a warm place for 15-20 minutes until frothy.

Sift the remaining flour, the salt, cinnamon and remaining sugar into a bowl. Rub in 2 oz. (¼ cup) of the butter. Make a well in the centre and pour in the yeast batter and the beaten eggs. Mix well to give a soft dough, adding more milk if necessary. Cover with a cloth and leave in a cool place for 50 minutes.

Soften the remaining butter and form into a rectangle, ½ inch thick. Knead the dough on a floured surface for 8 minutes then roll to a rectangle, 12 × 8 inches. Place the butter in the centre and fold the dough over to encase the butter.

Roll to an oblong, 5 × 15 inches. Fold evenly into three. Place in a polythene (plastic) bag and leave to rest in a cool place for 10 minutes. Repeat the rolling, folding and resting twice more. Chill for 1 hour.

Combine all the filling ingredients together in a bowl. Roll the dough to a rectangle, approximately ¼ inch thick and 16 inches long. Spread evenly with the filling, leaving a ½ inch border around the edge. Roll up tightly, as for a Swiss (jelly) roll. Place on a large, greased baking sheet and put inside an oiled polythene (plastic) bag. Leave in a warm place for 2 hours until well risen, then remove the bag.

Brush the roll with the glaze. Bake in a hot oven, 425°F, Gas Mark 7 for 20 minutes. Reduce the temperature to 350°F, Gas Mark 4 and bake for a further 20-25 minutes until golden brown. Turn onto a wire rack and cool completely before serving.
Makes one 16 inch roll

Christmas Candle Ring

½ oz. (½ cake) fresh (compressed)
  yeast
4 tablespoons (⅓ cup) warm
  water
1 lb. (4 cups) strong plain
  (all-purpose) flour
1 teaspoon salt
2 oz. (¼ cup) butter
¼ pint (⅔ cup) warm milk
3 oz. (½ cup) crystallized (candied)
  orange slices, chopped
2 oz. (⅓ cup) crystallized (candied)
  pineapple, chopped
1 oz. (¼ cup) almonds, chopped

1 oz. (3T) soft (light) brown sugar
½ teaspoon ground cinnamon
Glaze:
1 egg, beaten
1 teaspoon castor sugar
1 tablespoon water
Icing and decoration:
4 oz. (1 cup) icing (confectioners')
  sugar
1 tablespoon hot water
  (approximately)
few crystallized (candied) orange
  slices, cut into triangles
candle and holly leaves

Cream the yeast with the water. Sift the flour and salt into a warmed bowl and rub in the butter. Make a well in the centre and pour in the milk and yeast liquid. Using one hand or a spatula, draw the dry ingredients into the liquid and beat until the dough comes cleanly away from the sides of the bowl.

Turn onto a lightly floured surface and knead for 10 minutes until the dough is smooth and elastic. Place in a clean bowl, cover with a damp cloth and leave in a warm place for 1½ hours or until doubled in size.

Turn onto a lightly floured surface and knead lightly for 2 minutes. Divide in half and roll each piece of dough to a rectangle, about 12 × 5 inches.

Combine the crystallized fruit, almonds, sugar and cinnamon and spread over both pieces of dough. Roll up each one as for a Swiss (jelly) roll and seal the edges with water. Twist both rolls together and shape into a ring. Seal the ends with water.

Place the ring on a greased baking sheet and put a greased dariole mould in the centre. Put inside an oiled polythene (plastic) bag and leave in a warm place for 30 minutes or until doubled in size. Remove from the bag.

Beat together the ingredients for the glaze and brush over the risen dough. Bake in a moderately hot oven, 400°F, Gas Mark 6 for 40-45 minutes until golden brown. Turn onto a wire rack to cool.

Blend the icing sugar with enough hot water to give a smooth spreading consistency. Spoon the icing over the tea ring. Decorate with crystallized orange pieces. Place a candle in the dariole mould and surround with holly.
Makes one tea ring

INDIVIDUAL YEAST CAKES AND BUNS

Mincemeat Pinwheel Buns

½ oz. (½ cake) fresh (compressed)
  yeast
4 tablespoons (⅓ cup) warm
  water
8 oz. (2 cups) strong plain
  (all-purpose) flour
1 teaspoon salt
1½ oz. (3T) castor sugar
grated rind and juice of ½ orange

1 egg, beaten
Filling:
4 tablespoons (⅓ cup) mincemeat
1 large cooking apple, peeled,
  cored and coarsely grated
Glaze:
2 tablespoons (3T) clear honey,
  warmed

Cream the yeast with the water. Sift the flour and salt into a warmed bowl and stir in the sugar and orange rind. Make a well in the centre and pour in the beaten egg, orange juice and the yeast liquid. Using one hand or a spatula, draw the ingredients together and beat to give a firm dough that comes cleanly away from the sides of the bowl.

Turn onto a lightly floured surface and knead for 4 minutes until smooth and elastic. Place in a clean bowl, cover with a damp cloth and leave in a warm place for 1 hour or until doubled in size.

Turn onto a lightly floured surface and knead for 2 minutes. Roll to a rectangle, 6 × 12 inches. Mix together the mincemeat and apple and spread over the dough, leaving a ½ inch border around the edge. Roll up as for a Swiss (jelly) roll:

Cut into ½ inch slices and place in greased bun tins. Stand the tins on baking sheets. Put into oiled polythene (plastic) bags and leave in a warm place for 30 minutes until doubled in size. Remove from the bags.

Bake in a moderately hot oven, 400°F, Gas Mark 6 for 20-30 minutes, until golden brown. Whilst still warm, brush with honey, then turn out onto a wire rack and leave to cool.
Makes about 12 buns

Date Rolls

½ oz. (½ cake) fresh (compressed) yeast
2 oz. (⅓ cup) soft (light) brown sugar
½ pint (1 ¼ cups) warm milk
1 lb. (4 cups) strong plain (all-purpose) flour

1 teaspoon salt
¼ teaspoon ground cinnamon
¼ teaspoon mixed spice
grated rind and juice of 1 orange
4 oz. (½ cup) butter, softened
6 oz. (1 cup) stoned (pitted) dates, chopped

Blend the yeast with 1 teaspoon of the sugar, the milk and 4 oz. (1 cup) of the flour. Leave in a warm place for 15-20 minutes until frothy.

Sift the remaining flour, the salt and spices together into a warmed bowl. Stir in the orange rind. Make a well in the centre and pour in the orange juice and the yeast mixture. Using one hand or a spatula, draw all the ingredients together and continue to mix until the dough comes away from the sides of the bowl.

Turn onto a floured surface and knead well for 5-7 minutes. Put into a clean bowl, cover with a damp cloth and leave in a warm place for 1½ hours until doubled in size.

Knead the dough for 4 minutes, then roll to a rectangle, about ½ inch thick. Spread with the butter and sprinkle with the dates and remaining sugar. Roll up tightly as for a Swiss (jelly) roll. With a sharp knife cut into 1 inch slices. Place cut side down, ½ inch apart, on a large greased baking sheet.

Put into an oiled polythene (plastic) bag and leave in a warm place for 20 minutes or until doubled in size. Remove from the bag. Bake in a hot oven, 425°F, Gas Mark 7 for 15 minutes. Using a palette knife or spatula turn the slices over and bake for a further 10 minutes until well risen and golden brown. Cool on a wire rack for 10 minutes and serve warm or cold.
Makes 12 rolls

Apricot Kolachky

6 oz. (1 cup) dried apricots, finely
  chopped
3 tablespoons (¼ cup) sweet white
  wine, warmed
½ oz. (½ cake) fresh (compressed)
  yeast
2 oz. (¼ cup) castor (superfine)
  sugar

½ pint (1¼ cups) warm milk
1 lb. (4 cups) strong plain
  (all-purpose) flour
1 teaspoon salt
3 oz. (⅓ cup) butter, melted

Soak the apricots in the wine for 30 minutes. Drain and reserve the wine.
Blend the yeast with ½ teaspoon of the sugar, the milk and 4 oz. (1 cup) of
the flour. Leave in a warm place for 15-20 minutes or until frothy.

Sift the remaining flour and salt into a warmed bowl and stir in the rest of
the sugar. Form a well in the centre and pour in the yeast batter, reserved
wine and 2 oz. (¼ cup) of the butter. Using one hand or a spatula, blend
the ingredients together and beat until the dough is smooth.

Turn onto a lightly floured surface and knead for 5-7 minutes. Place in a
clean bowl, cover with a damp cloth and leave in a warm place for 1½-2
hours until doubled in size.

Turn onto a floured surface and lightly roll the dough out to a circle.
Sprinkle with the apricots. Fold the dough to enclose the fruit and knead
for 8 minutes.

Break the dough into 24 small pieces and form each into a ball. Place in
greased patty tins and stand on baking sheets. Put into oiled polythene
(plastic) bags. Leave in a warm place for 45 minutes or until doubled in
size. Remove from the bags.

Brush the dough with the remaining melted butter and bake in a hot
oven, 425°F, Gas Mark 7 for 15-20 minutes, until golden. Cool on a wire
rack before serving.
Makes 24 buns

Easter Men

1 oz. (1 cake) fresh (compressed)
   yeast
1 teaspoon castor (superfine)
   sugar
1 pint (2½ cups) warm milk
2 lb. (8 cups) strong plain
   (all-purpose) flour

1 teaspoon salt
1 oz. (2T) butter
6 eggs
12 currants
few slivered almonds, toasted
2-3 glacé (candied) cherries, sliced
beaten egg to glaze

Blend the yeast with the sugar, milk and 8 oz. (2 cups) of the flour. Leave in a warm place for 15-20 minutes until frothy.

Sift the remaining flour and salt into a warmed bowl and rub in the butter. Make a well in the centre and pour in the yeast mixture. Using one hand, mix thoroughly and beat until the dough comes cleanly away from the sides of the bowl.

Turn onto a lightly floured surface and knead for 3 minutes. Place in a bowl, cover with a damp cloth and leave in a warm place for 1 hour or until doubled in size.

Turn onto a lightly floured surface and knead for 4 minutes. Divide the dough into 6 pieces and form each into an oblong. Place a raw, unshelled egg in the centre of each piece.

Imagine the egg is a clock face and make slits in the dough at 2, 4, 6, 8 and 10 o'clock. Shape the dough to form arms, legs and a head. Use currants to make eyes, almonds for the nose and cherries for the mouth. Fold the arms over the egg.

Place on greased baking sheets, put inside oiled polythene (plastic) bags and leave in a warm place for 20-30 minutes until puffy. Remove from the bag and brush with egg glaze. Bake in a hot oven, 450°F, Gas Mark 8 for 30 minutes until golden brown.

Serve warm with butter.

Makes 6

EASTER MEN *(Photograph: Dutch Dairy Bureau)*

Fruit Buns with Walnut Syrup

1 oz. (1 cake) fresh (compressed)
  yeast
5 tablespoons (6T) warm water
¼ pint + 4 tablespoons (1 cup)
  warm milk
4 oz. (½ cup) castor (superfine)
  sugar
1¼ lb. (5 cups) strong plain
  (all-purpose) flour
½ teaspoon salt
1 teaspoon ground cinnamon
grated rind and juice of 1 lemon

4 oz. (⅔ cup) currants
4 oz. (⅔ cup) sultanas (seedless
  white raisins)
2 egg yolks
3 oz. (⅓ cup) butter, softened
Syrup:
12 oz. (2 cups) soft (light) brown
  sugar
6 tablespoons (½ cup) water
2 oz. (¼ cup) butter
3 oz. (¾ cup) walnuts, finely
  chopped

Blend the yeast with the water, milk, 1 teaspoon of the sugar and 5 oz.
(1¼ cups) of the flour. Leave in a warm place for 15 minutes until frothy.

Sift the remaining flour, the salt and cinnamon into a warmed bowl. Stir
in the remaining sugar, the lemon rind, juice and the dried fruit. Make a
well in the centre and pour in the yeast batter and egg yolks. Add the
softened butter and mix all the ingredients together until evenly blended.

Turn onto a floured surface and knead for 5-7 minutes until smooth and
elastic. Put into a clean bowl, cover with a damp cloth and leave in a warm
place for 1½-2 hours until doubled in bulk.

Prepare the syrup by dissolving the sugar in the water over gentle heat.
Increase the heat and boil until the temperature reaches 230°F. Remove
from the heat and allow to cool for 3 minutes. Stir in the butter and
chopped nuts. Cover and keep warm.

Knead the dough on a floured surface for 5 minutes. Roll out to ½ inch
thickness. With a 2½ inch plain pastry cutter, cut out 24 circles of dough.
Place 12 of the circles on a greased baking sheet. Brush with some of the
warm syrup. Cover with the other circles, pressing together gently but
firmly. Brush with the remaining syrup.

Leave to rise in a warm place for 20 minutes or until doubled in size.
Bake in a hot oven, 425°F, Gas Mark 7 for 25 minutes or until golden
brown. Transfer to a wire rack to cool. Serve warm or cold.
Makes 12 buns

Almond Fingers

½ oz. (½ cake) fresh (compressed)
  yeast
5 tablespoons (6T) warm water
1 oz. (2T) castor (superfine) sugar
8 oz. (2 cups) strong plain
  (all-purpose) flour
½ teaspoon salt
1 oz. (2T) lard (shortening)
1 egg, beaten

5 oz. (⅔ cup) butter
12 oz. marzipan
beaten egg to glaze
Icing and decoration:
6 oz. (1 ⅓ cups) icing
  (confectioners') sugar
1-2 tablespoons warm water
glacé (candied) cherries, chopped

Blend the yeast with the water, 1 teaspoon of the sugar and 2 oz. (½ cup) of the flour. Leave in a warm place for about 15 minutes or until frothy.

Sift the remaining flour and salt into a bowl and stir in the rest of the sugar. Rub in the lard. Form a well in the centre and pour in the yeast mixture and beaten egg. Draw all the ingredients together and mix until smooth.

Turn onto a lightly floured surface and knead for 5 minutes until the dough is elastic in texture. Cover with a damp cloth and leave in a cool place for 10 minutes.

Shape the butter into an oblong, 9 × 3 inches. Roll the dough to a 10 inch square and place the butter in the centre. Fold the sides over and seal.

Roll to an oblong, about 15 × 5 inches. Fold the top third of the dough down and the bottom third up. Put into an oiled polythene (plastic) bag and leave in a cool place for 10 minutes. Repeat rolling and folding twice more. Finally rest the dough for 30 minutes in a cool place then roll out to a 12 × 8 inch rectangle. Cut into 12 strips, 1 inch wide.

Divide the marzipan into 12 pieces and form into finger shapes. Wrap the pastry dough around the marzipan. Place on a greased baking sheet, put into an oiled polythene (plastic) bag and leave in a warm place for 30 minutes until slightly risen and spongy. Remove from the bag. Brush with beaten egg and bake in a hot oven, 425°F, Gas Mark 7 for 15-20 minutes.

Transfer to a wire rack. Blend the icing sugar with enough warm water to give a smooth, coating consistency, glacé icing. Spread over the almond fingers while still warm. Sprinkle with the cherries.
Makes 12 fingers

ENRICHED DOUGHS

Croissants

scant ½ oz. (½ cake) fresh
  (compressed) yeast
¼ pint (⅔ cup) warm milk
  (approximately)
12 oz. (3 cups) strong plain
  (all-purpose) flour, sifted
½ teaspoon salt

1 tablespoon castor (superfine)
  sugar
6 oz. (¾ cup) butter
Glaze:
1 egg, lightly beaten
½ teaspoon sugar

Cream the yeast with 2 tablespoons (3T) of the milk. Blend with 3 oz.
(¾ cup) flour to form a soft dough. Drop this ball of dough into a large bowl
of warm water. Leave to become 'spongy', about 20 minutes.

Add the salt and sugar to the remaining flour. Make a well in the centre.
Soften 3 oz. (⅓ cup) of the butter and mix into the dry ingredients with
enough of the milk to form a soft dough. Beat on a board for 5 minutes
until the dough is smooth and elastic. Flatten the dough.

Carefully lift the yeast ball from the water, using a slotted spoon. Drain
and place in the centre of the dough. Knead well. Put the dough into a
floured bowl, cover and chill for 12 hours. Chill the rest of the butter.

Roll the dough into a rectangle and place the butter in the centre. Fold
one third of the dough over the butter and the other third of the dough on
top. Turn the dough so that the folded end is on the right-hand side. Roll
out to an oblong again, fold into 3 and turn. Repeat once more. Place in a
greased polythene (plastic) bag and chill in the refrigerator for 30 minutes.

Roll out the dough as before, to a rectangle. Repeat folding, turning and
rolling twice more. Chill in the refrigerator for 30 minutes.

To shape the croissants, roll the dough into a rectangle, about 21 × 12
inches. Using a sharp knife, trim the edges and cut in half lengthwise. Cut
each strip into triangles, 6 inches high, with a 6 inch base.

Beat the egg with the sugar and a few drops of water. Brush over the
triangles then roll up loosely, beginning at the base and finishing with the
tip underneath. Curve into crescent shapes.

Place well apart on dampened baking sheets and put into oiled
polythene (plastic) bags. Leave in a warm place for about 30 minutes until
light and puffy. Remove from the bags.

Brush the croissants with egg glaze and bake in a hot oven, 425°F, Gas
Mark 7 for 15-20 minutes until golden brown. Cool slightly on a wire rack
before serving the croissants warm.
Makes 12 croissants

CROISSANTS *(Photograph: Lintas London)*

Date and Orange Rolls

½ oz. (½ cake) fresh (compressed)
 yeast
3 tablespoons (¼ cup) warm milk
1 lb. (4 cups) strong plain
 (all-purpose) flour
1 teaspoon salt
4 oz. (½ cup) castor (superfine)
 sugar
3 tablespoons (¼ cup) soured
 cream
2 tablespoons (3T) orange juice
6 oz. (¾ cup) butter, melted
2 eggs, lightly beaten

3 oz. (½ cup) stoned (pitted)
 dates, chopped
grated rind of 2 large oranges
1 oz. (3T) mixed (candied) peel,
 chopped
¼ teaspoon ground cinnamon
¼ teaspoon mixed spice
Icing:
8 oz. (1¾ cups) icing
 (confectioners') sugar
2 tablespoons (3T) orange juice
 (approximately)

Cream the yeast with the milk. Sift the flour and salt into a warmed bowl. Stir in 2 oz. (¼ cup) of the sugar. Make a well in the centre and pour in the yeast liquid, soured cream, orange juice, 5 oz. (⅔ cup) of the butter and the beaten eggs. Using one hand or a spatula, draw the flour into the liquid and beat until the mixture comes cleanly away from the sides of the bowl.

Turn onto a lightly floured surface and knead for 10 minutes until the dough is smooth and elastic. Place in a clean bowl, cover with a damp cloth and leave to rise in a warm place for 1½ hours or until doubled in size.

Knead for 2 minutes on a floured surface, then roll to a 12 inch square. Brush with the remaining butter. Combine the dates, orange rind, peel and spices together with the remaining 2 oz. (¼ cup) of sugar. Sprinkle evenly over the dough, leaving a ½ inch border around the edge. Roll up as for a Swiss (jelly) roll.

With a sharp knife, cut into 1½ inch slices and place close together, but not quite touching, on a baking sheet. Put into an oiled polythene (plastic) bag and leave in a warm place for 30-35 minutes until risen and touching. Remove from the bag. Bake in a moderately hot oven, 375°F, Gas Mark 5 for 30-35 minutes until golden brown.

Prepare the icing by blending the icing sugar with sufficient orange juice to give a smooth coating consistency. Coat the warm buns with the icing and leave until cool enough to handle before lifting onto a wire rack. Allow to cool and separate the buns before serving.
Makes 12-15 buns

Brioches

8 oz. (2 cups) strong plain
  (all-purpose) flour
½ teaspoon salt
1 tablespoon castor (superfine)
  sugar
½ oz. (½ cake) fresh (compressed)
  yeast

3 tablespoons (¼ cup) warm
  water
2 eggs, beaten
4 oz. (½ cup) butter, melted

Sift the flour and salt into a warmed bowl. Stir in the sugar. Cream the yeast with the water. Stir the yeast liquid, beaten eggs and the melted butter into the dry ingredients with a wooden spoon. Beat until smooth and elastic in texture. Cover with a damp cloth and leave in a warm place for 1½-2 hours until doubled in size.

Divide the risen dough between 8 well-greased fluted brioche tins. Bake in the centre of a hot oven, 425°F, Gas Mark 7 for 10 minutes until golden brown.

Cool in the tin for 20 minutes before turning onto a wire rack.

Makes 8-10 brioches

Savoury Brioches

8 oz. (2 cups) strong plain
  (all-purpose) flour
¼ teaspoon salt
freshly ground black pepper
½ oz. (½ cake) fresh (compressed)
  yeast
3 tablespoons (¼ cup) warm
  water

¼ teaspoon French mustard
4 oz. (½ cup) butter, melted
2 oz. (½ cup) Gruyère cheese,
  finely grated
2 eggs, lightly beaten

Sift the flour, salt and pepper into a warmed bowl. Make a well in the centre. Cream the yeast with the water. Add the mustard, butter, cheese, eggs and yeast liquid to the flour and beat with a wooden spoon to produce a smooth batter. Cover with a damp cloth and leave in a warm place for 1½-2 hours until doubled in bulk.

Pour into 8 individual greased fluted brioche tins. Bake in the centre of a hot oven, 425°F, Gas Mark 7 for 10-15 minutes until golden brown.

Allow to cool in the tins for 5 minutes before turning out. Serve warm or cold.

Makes 8 brioches

Danish Pastries

Pastry dough:
1 oz. (1 cake) fresh (compressed)
  yeast
¼ pint (⅔ cup) warm milk
1 lb. (4 cups) plain (all-purpose)
  flour
1 teaspoon salt
10 oz. (1¼ cups) butter
2 oz. (¼ cup) castor sugar
2 eggs, beaten
beaten egg to glaze

Filling:
1 oz. (2T) butter
3 oz. (⅓ cup) castor sugar
3 oz. (¾ cup) ground almonds
½ beaten egg
Icing and decoration:
8 oz. (1¾ cups) icing
  (confectioners') sugar
1-2 tablespoons hot water
chopped nuts
few glacé (candied) cherries

Cream the yeast with 2 tablespoons (3T) of the milk. Sift flour and salt into a bowl. Rub in 2 oz. (¼ cup) of the butter. Stir in the sugar. Make a well in the centre and pour in the yeast liquid, remaining milk and beaten eggs. Beat thoroughly to give a soft dough, adding more milk if necessary.

Flatten the remaining butter to an oblong, 9 × 5 inches. Knead the dough on a floured surface until smooth and elastic then roll out to a 10-11 inch square. Place the butter in the centre and fold the dough over, encasing the butter. Roll to an oblong, about 8 × 24 inches. Fold the dough into 3 and place in a polythene (plastic) bag. Leave to rest in the refrigerator for 15 minutes. Repeat the rolling, folding and resting three times.

To prepare the filling, cream the butter with the sugar, almonds and egg to give a stiff paste. Roll out the chilled dough to a large rectangle, about ¼ inch thick. To make envelope pastries, cut into 4 inch squares. Place a little filling in the centre of each square. Fold the corners into the centre, enclosing the filling. Place the pastries on baking sheets and cover with greased polythene (plastic) sheets. Leave in a warm place for 20 minutes. Bake above the centre of a hot oven, 425°F, Gas Mark 7 for 12-15 minutes.

Blend the icing sugar with enough hot water to give a coating consistency. Spread on top of the pastries. Top with chopped nuts and glacé cherries.
Makes 12-15 pastries

Stars:
Make the pastry dough and filling as above. Cut the dough into 3 inch squares and place a small amount of filling in the centre of each one. Make sharp cuts from the corners to within ½ inch of the centre. Fold alternate corners to the centre, overlapping each other. Continue as above.

Cinnamon Knots

½ oz. (½ cake) fresh (compressed) yeast
4 tablespoons (⅓ cup) warm milk
8 oz. (2 cups) strong plain (all-purpose) flour
½ teaspoon salt
1 oz. (2T) butter or margarine
1 egg, beaten
oil for deep frying
2 oz. (¼ cup) castor (superfine) sugar
1 teaspoon ground cinnamon

Cream the yeast with the milk. Sift the flour and salt into a warmed bowl and rub in the fat. Make a well in the centre and pour in the yeast liquid and beaten egg. Mix to a soft but manageable dough, adding more milk if necessary. Cover with a damp cloth and leave in a warm place for 1 hour.

Turn onto a floured surface and knead for 3 minutes. Divide into 8 pieces and shape each into a roll, about 7 inches long. Tie into a knot. Place on warmed, greased baking sheets. Put into large polythene (plastic) bags and leave in a warm place for about 15-20 minutes or until puffy.

Heat the oil in a deep fryer to 375°F. Fry the knots in the hot oil for 4-5 minutes or until golden. Drain on kitchen paper. Mix together the sugar and cinnamon and toss the knots in this mixture. Serve warm.

Makes 8 knots

Doughnuts with Lemon

½ oz. (½ cake) fresh (compressed) yeast
5 tablespoons (6T) warm milk
8 oz. (2 cups) strong plain (all-purpose) flour
½ teaspoon salt
¼ teaspoon grated nutmeg
1 oz. (2T) castor (superfine) sugar
grated rind and juice of 1 lemon
2 oz. (¼ cup) butter, melted
1 egg, lightly beaten
oil for deep frying
castor (superfine) sugar for dusting

Cream the yeast with the milk. Sift the flour, salt and nutmeg into a warmed bowl. Stir in the sugar and lemon rind. Make a well in the centre and pour in the lemon juice, melted butter, beaten egg and the yeast liquid. Beat until the dough comes cleanly away from the sides of the bowl.

Turn onto a lightly floured surface and knead for 5 minutes until the dough is no longer sticky, but smooth and elastic in texture. Put into a clean bowl, cover and leave in a warm place until doubled in bulk.

Turn onto a floured surface and knead for 4 minutes. Roll the dough out to ¼ inch thickness. Cut out circles, using a 3 inch plain cutter. With a 1 inch plain cutter, remove the centres from the circles, forming rings. Place on a greased baking sheet, spacing apart. Place in an oiled polythene (plastic) bag and leave in a warm place for 15-20 minutes until puffy.

Heat the oil in a deep fryer until it reaches 375°F. Gently lower in the doughnuts, a few at a time, and fry for about 4 minutes until golden brown. Drain on kitchen paper, toss in the sugar and serve warm.

Makes about 12 doughnuts

Austrian Jam Doughnuts

½ oz. (½ cake) fresh (compressed)
  yeast
1 tablespoon warm water
1 lb. (4 cups) strong plain
  (all-purpose) flour
¼ teaspoon salt
3 tablespoons (¼ cup) castor
  (superfine) sugar
1 teaspoon grated orange rind

6 egg yolks, beaten
¼ pint (⅔ cup) single (light)
  cream, warmed
1 tablespoon rum
1 teaspoon vanilla essence
apricot jam for filling
oil for deep frying
icing (confectioners') sugar for
  dusting

Blend the yeast with the water. Sift the flour and salt into a warmed bowl. Stir in the sugar and orange rind. Make a well in the centre and pour in the egg yolks, cream, rum, vanilla essence and yeast liquid. Draw all the ingredients together until evenly incorporated and mix to a smooth dough.

Place in a well greased bowl. Cover with a damp cloth and set aside in a warm place for 1½-2 hours or until doubled in size.

Punch the dough down in the bowl to deflate it, then turn onto a lightly floured surface. Roll into a large circle, about ¼ inch thick. With a lightly floured 3 inch plain pastry cutter, cut out circles of dough.

Place 1 teaspoon jam on the centre of half of the circles. Cover each with a plain circle of dough and press the edges together. With a slightly smaller cutter, trim off the rough edges. Place 1 inch apart on lightly greased and floured baking sheets. Put inside oiled polythene (plastic) bags and leave in a warm place for 30 minutes until puffy.

Heat the oil in a deep fryer to 375°F or until hot enough to turn a cube of stale bread golden in 20-30 seconds. Fry the doughnuts, a few at a time, turning occasionally, for 3 minutes or until golden brown. Drain on kitchen paper. Dust with icing sugar before serving.

Makes about 24 doughnuts

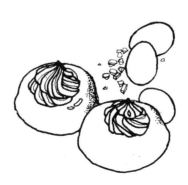

Oliebollen

¾ oz. (¾ cake) fresh (compressed)
  yeast
½ pint (1¼ cups) warm milk
1 lb. (4 cups) strong plain
  (all-purpose) flour
1 teaspoon salt
2 eggs, beaten

8 oz. (1⅓ cups) currants
1 oz. (3T) mixed (candied) peel,
  chopped
1 small dessert apple, peeled,
  cored and finely chopped
oil for deep frying
castor (superfine) sugar for dusting

Cream the yeast with 3 tablespoons (¼ cup) of the milk. Sift flour and salt into a warmed bowl and form a well in the centre. Pour in the yeast liquid, remaining milk and the beaten eggs. Draw the ingredients together and beat until the dough comes cleanly away from the sides of the bowl.

Turn onto a lightly floured surface and knead in the currants, peel and apple. Continue to knead until the dough is smooth and elastic. Put into a bowl, cover with a damp cloth and leave in a warm place for 1 hour until doubled in size.

Heat the oil in a deep fryer to 375°F, or until hot enough to turn a cube of stale bread golden in 20-30 seconds. Using a greased tablespoon, drop small balls of the mixture into the oil and fry for about 4 minutes until golden brown. Remove and drain on kitchen paper. Sprinkle with sugar before serving.

Makes about 25 oliebollen

Gougnettes

½ oz. (½ cake) fresh (compressed)
  yeast
1 tablespoon warm water
1 lb. (4 cups) strong plain
  (all-purpose) flour
1 teaspoon salt

2 oz. (¼ cup) castor (superfine)
  sugar
5 eggs, well beaten
3 oz. (⅓ cup) butter
6 tablespoons (½ cup) oil

Cream the yeast with the water. Sift flour and salt into a warmed mixing bowl. Stir in the sugar. Form a well in the centre and pour in the eggs and yeast liquid. Draw the dry ingredients into the liquid and continue mixing until the dough comes away from the sides of the bowl.

Turn onto a lightly floured board and knead for 3-4 minutes to yield a smooth, elastic dough. Shape into a ball and place in a bowl. Cover with a damp cloth and leave in a warm place until almost doubled in bulk.

Knead well for about 8 minutes on a lightly floured surface. Roll out to an oblong, ¾ inch thick. Cut into 2 inch wide strips. Roll each strip into a sausage and cut into 1 inch pieces. Leave to rest for 10-15 minutes.

Heat butter and oil in a frying pan (skillet) over moderate heat. Fry the pieces of dough for 2-3 minutes on each side until crisp and golden brown. Drain on kitchen paper and serve immediately.

Makes about 50 gougnettes

OLIEBOLLEN *(Photograph: Dutch Dairy Bureau)*

Rum Babas

1 oz. (1 cake) fresh (compressed)
  yeast
6 tablespoons (½ cup) warm milk
8 oz. (2 cups) strong plain
  (all-purpose) flour
½ teaspoon salt
1½ oz. (3T) castor (superfine)
  sugar
4 eggs, beaten
4 oz. (½ cup) butter, softened
Syrup:
8 oz. (1 cup) sugar
½ pint (1¼ cups) water
grated rind and juice of 1 large
  orange

4 tablespoons (⅓ cup) clear honey
5 tablespoons (6T) rum
Filling:
3 oranges, peeled, pith removed
  and segmented
3 bananas, sliced and sprinkled
  with lemon juice
4 oz. (1 cup) grapes, halved and
  deseeded
Glaze:
5 tablespoons (6T) clear honey,
  warmed

Blend the yeast with the milk and 2 oz. (½ cup) of the flour in a large bowl. Leave in a warm place for 20 minutes or until frothy.

Sift the remaining flour and salt into the yeast mixture and stir in the sugar and beaten eggs. Add the softened butter and work the ingredients together, using a wooden spoon. Beat for 3-4 minutes to give a smooth, soft dough.

Divide the mixture between 12-16 greased individual ring moulds. The tins should only be half full. Place on baking sheets, put into oiled polythene (plastic) bags and leave in a warm place for 30-40 minutes until risen to the top of the moulds. Remove from the bag. Bake in a moderately hot oven, 400°F, Gas Mark 6 for 10-15 minutes until golden brown.

Meanwhile, prepare the syrup by dissolving the sugar in the water in a heavy saucepan over a gentle heat. When the sugar has dissolved, bring to the boil and boil for 1 minute. Take off the heat and stir in the orange rind, juice, honey and rum.

Turn the cooked babas onto a wire tray placed over a plate. Set aside 4 tablespoons (⅓ cup) of the syrup. Spoon the remainder over the warm babas until it has soaked through. Allow to cool.

When cold, place on serving plates. Mix the fruit with the reserved syrup and pile into the centres of the babas. Brush with the honey glaze.
Makes 12-16 babas

Note: If preferred, the babas may be filled with piped swirls of whipped cream instead of fruit.

Apricot Fritters

¼ oz. (¼ cake) fresh (compressed)
 yeast
¼ pint + 2 tablespoons (¾ cup)
 warm milk
6 oz. (1 ½ cups) strong plain
 (all-purpose) flour
¼ teaspoon salt
1 oz. (2T) butter, melted
15 oz. can apricot halves
oil for deep frying
castor (superfine) sugar for dusting
½ teaspoon ground cinnamon

Cream the yeast with 2 tablespoons (3T) of the milk. Sift the flour and salt into a warmed bowl. Make a well in the centre and pour in the yeast liquid and remaining milk. Beat thoroughly. Cover and leave in a warm place for 1-1½ hours until doubled in size.

Stir in the melted butter and beat for 3 minutes. Cover and leave to rise in a warm place for 30 minutes. Coat the apricots in batter, place on well-greased sheets of greaseproof (waxed) paper and leave in a warm place for 30 minutes until puffy.

Heat the oil in a deep fryer to 375°F. Lower the fritters into the hot oil and deep fry for 4-5 minutes until golden brown. Drain and dredge with castor sugar. Sprinkle with cinnamon.

Makes about 12 fritters

Blackberry Yeast Pancakes

½ oz. (½ cake) fresh (compressed)
 yeast
½ pint (1 ¼ cups) warm milk
10 oz. (2 ¼ cups) strong plain
 (all-purpose) flour
¼ teaspoon salt
2 oz. (¼ cup) castor (superfine)
 sugar
2 eggs, lightly beaten
3 oz. (⅓ cup) butter, melted
1 lb. (4 cups) blackberries, washed
 and hulled
2 tablespoons (3T) icing
 (confectioners') sugar
½ pint (1 ¼ cups) soured cream,
 warmed

Cream the yeast with 2 tablespoons (3T) of the milk. Sift flour and salt into a warmed bowl. Stir in the sugar. Make a well in the centre and pour in the yeast liquid, remaining milk, beaten eggs and 1 oz. (2T) of the melted butter. Gradually draw the ingredients together and beat to form a smooth batter. Cover and leave in a warm place for 30 minutes.

Heat the remaining butter in a frying pan (skillet) over moderate heat. Drop tablespoonfuls of batter into the pan and fry on each side for 30 seconds or until golden brown.

Transfer to a warmed serving plate, fold in half, then fold again to give a fan shape. Tuck the blackberries into the pockets. Keep the pancakes warm whilst cooking the remainder.

Sprinkle icing sugar over the pancakes and pour a little cream over. Serve the rest separately.

Serves 6

SAVOURY DOUGHS

Pizza Napoletana

Pizza dough:
1 lb. (4 cups) strong plain
  (all-purpose) flour
1 teaspoon salt
½ oz. (½ cake) fresh (compressed)
  yeast
½ pint (1¼ cups) warm water
Topping:
15 oz. can tomatoes, drained and
  chopped

1 clove garlic, crushed
½ teaspoon dried mixed herbs
½ teaspoon dried oregano
8 oz. Mozzarella cheese, sliced
3 oz. (½ cup) stuffed green olives,
  sliced
1 can anchovy fillets, drained
salt
freshly ground black pepper
1 tablespoon olive oil

Sift the flour and salt into a warmed bowl and make a well in the centre.
Cream the yeast with 2 tablespoons (3T) of the water. Pour the yeast liquid
and remaining water into the flour. Work the dough, using one hand, until
it leaves the sides of the bowl clean.

Turn onto a lightly floured surface and knead until smooth and elastic.
Shape into a ball and place in an oiled polythene (plastic) bag. Leave in a
warm place for about 1 hour or until doubled in size.

Turn onto a lightly floured surface and knead lightly for 2 minutes.
Divide the dough into 4 pieces and roll each to an 8 inch circle. Place on
greased baking sheets.

To prepare the topping, spread the tomatoes and garlic over the dough
to within ½ inch of the edge. Sprinkle with herbs and cover with cheese.
Arrange the olives and anchovies on top. Season well and brush with oil.

Bake in a hot oven, 425°F, Gas Mark 7 for 25 minutes. Pizza is best
eaten hot but can also be served cold.
Makes 4 pizzas

Pizza with mushrooms and bacon:
Prepare the basic pizza dough as above. For the topping, slice 2 large
onions and 4 oz. (½ cup) mushrooms and sauté in 2 tablespoons (3T)
olive oil until soft. Allow to cool then spread over the dough to within
½ inch of the edge. Season well. Arrange strips of derinded bacon and
sliced stuffed olives on top. Bake as above.
Spicy prawn pizza:
Prepare the basic pizza dough as above. For the topping, blend together
4 oz. (½ cup) softened cream cheese, 2 tablespoons (3T) mango chutney
and ½ teaspoon curry powder. Stir in 3 oz. (½ cup) cooked shelled
prawns. Spread over the dough to within 1 inch of the edge. Arrange sliced
tomatoes in a ring on top and brush with oil. Bake as above. Garnish with a
sprig of fresh parsley.

PIZZA NAPOLETANA *(Photograph: Olives from Spain)*

Onion Kuchen

½ pint (1¼ cups) milk
4 oz. (½ cup) butter
½ oz. (½ cake) fresh (compressed)
  yeast
1 tablespoon warm water
1 lb. (4 cups) strong plain
  (all-purpose) flour
1½ teaspoons salt
1 tablespoon castor (superfine)
  sugar

2 tablespoons (3T) oil
1 lb (4 cups) onions, thinly sliced
6 slices streaky (fatty) bacon,
  derinded and diced
freshly ground black pepper
6 oz. cheese, preferably
  Mozzarella, thinly sliced

Place the milk and 2 oz. (¼ cup) butter in a saucepan and heat gently until the butter has melted. Cream the yeast with the water. Sift the flour and 1 teaspoon salt into a warmed bowl. Add the sugar. Make a well in the centre and pour in the yeast liquid and butter and milk mixture. Gradually draw the ingredients together, using one hand or a spatula, and beat to form a smooth, soft dough which comes away from the sides of the bowl.

Turn onto a lightly floured surface and knead for 10 minutes. Put into a clean bowl, cover with a damp cloth and set aside in a warm place for about 1½ hours or until the dough has doubled in size.

Turn onto a floured surface and work in the oil, kneading well for 5 minutes. Roll into a 9 inch circle and place on a large, greased baking sheet. Cover with a damp cloth and leave in a warm place for 45 minutes or until almost doubled in size.

Meanwhile, melt the remaining butter in a frying pan over moderate heat. Add the onions and cook, stirring occasionally, for 5-7 minutes until soft and translucent but not browned. Transfer to a bowl. Add the bacon to the pan and cook for 5 minutes, stirring frequently, until crisp. Drain on kitchen paper then add to the onions and mix well. Season with salt and pepper.

Spread the onion mixture over the risen dough. Arrange the cheese slices on top. Bake in the centre of a very hot oven 475°F, Gas Mark 9 for 15 minutes. Reduce the temperature to moderately hot, 375°F, Gas Mark 5 and transfer the baking sheet to a lower oven shelf. Continue baking for 20-25 minutes until the bread is golden brown and sounds hollow when tapped underneath.

Remove from the oven and allow to cool slightly before serving.
Makes one 9 inch round loaf

Rosemary Bread

½ oz. (½ cake) fresh (compressed)
  yeast
½ pint (1¼ cups) warm water
12 oz. (3 cups) strong plain
  (all-purpose) flour

1 teaspoon salt
4 oz. (1 cup) wholemeal
  (wholewheat) flour
4 teaspoons fresh rosemary,
  chopped

Cream the yeast with 2 tablespoons (3T) of the water. Sift the plain flour
and salt together into a warmed bowl. Stir in the wholemeal flour and 3
teaspoons of the rosemary. Make a well in the centre and pour in the yeast
liquid and the remaining water. Gradually draw the flours into the liquid
and continue mixing until all the ingredients are well blended and the
dough comes away from the sides of the bowl.

Turn the dough onto a lightly floured board and knead for 5 minutes to
form a smooth, elastic ball. Place in a clean bowl, cover with a sheet of
oiled polythene (plastic) and set aside for 1½-2 hours in a warm place until
the dough has doubled in size.

Turn the dough onto a lightly floured surface and knead for 3 minutes.
Shape into a loaf and place in a greased 1 lb. loaf tin. Put the tin into an
oiled polythene (plastic) bag and leave to rise in a warm place for about
45 minutes or until the dough has risen to the top of the tin. Sprinkle with
the remaining rosemary. Bake in the centre of a hot oven, 475°F, Gas
Mark 9 for 15 minutes. Lower the temperature to moderately hot, 375°F,
Gas Mark 5 and bake for a further 25 minutes.

Turn the loaf out of the tin and tap the base with the knuckles. If it sounds
hollow, the loaf is cooked, if not, place upside down on a baking sheet.
Return to the oven, lower the temperature to moderate, 325°F, Gas
Mark 3 and bake for a further 5-10 minutes. Cool on a wire rack.
Makes one 1 lb. loaf

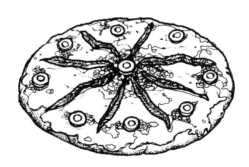

Cheese and Date Bread

8 oz. (2 cups) plain (all-purpose)
  flour
2 teaspoons baking powder
1 teaspoon dry mustard
½ teaspoon salt
freshly ground black pepper
2 oz. (¼ cup) butter or margarine

4 oz. (1 cup) Cheddar cheese,
  grated
2-3 oz. (½ cup) stoned (pitted)
  dates, chopped
2 eggs, beaten
¼ pint, (⅔ cup) milk

Sift the flour, baking powder, mustard, salt and pepper into a bowl. Rub in the butter or margarine. Stir in the grated cheese and chopped dates. Set aside 2 teaspoons of the beaten egg for brushing. Combine the remainder with the milk. Add to the dry ingredients and beat thoroughly.

Spoon the mixture into a greased and floured 1 lb. loaf tin. Brush with beaten egg. Bake in the centre of a moderately hot oven, 375°F, Gas Mark 5 for 45 minutes until golden brown and firm to the touch.

Serve either hot or cold, sliced and buttered.

Makes one 1 lb. loaf

Calzone

½ oz. (½ cake) fresh (compressed)
  yeast
½ pint (1¼ cups) warm water
1 lb. (4 cups) strong plain
  (all-purpose) flour
1½ teaspoons salt
1 oz. (2T) lard (shortening)

Filling:
8 slices cooked (processed) ham
8 slices Bel Paese cheese
2 tablespoons (3T) olive oil
freshly ground black pepper

Cream the yeast with 2 tablespoons (3T) of the water. Sift the flour and salt into a warmed bowl and rub in the lard. Make a well in the centre and pour in the yeast liquid and remaining water. Draw all the ingredients together and beat until the mixture comes cleanly away from the sides of the bowl.

Turn onto a lightly floured surface and knead well for 5 minutes until smooth and elastic. Place in a clean bowl, cover with a damp cloth and leave in a warm place for 1½ hours or until the dough has doubled in size.

Turn onto a lightly floured surface and knead for 2 minutes. Divide the dough into 8 pieces and roll each to a 6 inch circle.

Place a folded slice of ham and a slice of cheese on one half of each circle. Sprinkle with a little olive oil and season well. Brush the edges of the dough with water, fold to form a semi-circle, enclosing the filling. Press the edges together to seal.

Place on greased baking sheets and put into oiled polythene (plastic) bags. Leave in a warm place for 15 minutes until puffy. Remove from the bag. Bake in a hot oven, 425°F, Gas Mark 7 for 15-20 minutes. Serve warm.

Makes 8

Ploughman's Loaf

½ oz. (½ cake) fresh (compressed)
  yeast
½ pint (1 ¼ cups) warm milk
1 lb. (4 cups) strong plain
  (all-purpose) flour
salt
2 ½ oz. (5T) butter, melted

1 onion, thinly sliced
1 garlic clove, crushed (optional)
freshly ground black pepper
1 egg yolk
1 ½ tablespoons (2T) soured
  cream

Cream the yeast with 2 tablespoons (3T) of the milk. Sift the flour and
1 teaspoon salt into a warmed bowl and make a well in the centre. Pour in
the yeast liquid, remaining milk and 1½ oz. (3T) of the butter. Draw the
ingredients together and beat until the dough comes cleanly away from the
sides of the bowl.

Turn onto a lightly floured surface and knead for about 8 minutes until
the dough is smooth and elastic. Put into a clean bowl and cover with a
damp cloth. Leave in a warm place for 1½-2 hours until doubled in size.

Melt the remaining butter in a frying pan. Add the onion and garlic, if
used, and fry, stirring occasionally, for 5-7 minutes until soft and
translucent but not brown. Season with salt and pepper. Take out of the
pan, using a slotted spoon, and spread evenly over the base of a
well-greased 8 inch round cake tin. Reserve the butter in the pan.

Knead the dough for 4 minutes, then roll to an 8 inch circle. Place
carefully over the onions, pressing it well to the sides of the tin. Brush with
the reserved butter. Put into an oiled polythene (plastic) bag and leave to
rise in a warm place for 30-40 minutes until doubled in bulk. Remove from
the bag.

Beat the egg yolk with the soured cream, salt and pepper. Sprinkle over
the dough and bake in the centre of a hot oven 425°F, Gas Mark 7 for
10 minutes. Lower the temperature to moderately hot, 375°F, Gas Mark 5
and bake for a further 20 minutes. Turn onto a wire rack to cool
completely before serving with cheese.

Serves 5-6

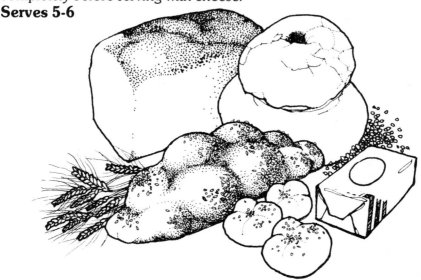

INDEX

INDEX

PDO 80-192